MW01658019

Collecting Vintage Men's Magazines

Collecting Vintage Men's Magazines

By
Todd Frye

Published by
Todd Frye
Harrogate, Tennessee

Collecting Vintage Men's Magazines

Published by:
Todd Frye
PO Box 577
Harrogate TN 37752
toddfrye@yahoo.com

All rights reserved. No part of the text of this book may be reproduced or transmitted in any form or by any means, electronic or mechanical, including photocopying, recording, or by any information storage and retrieval system, without prior written permission of the author, except for the inclusion of brief quotations for the purposes of review.

Copyright 2013 by Todd Frye.

ISBN-13: 978-0-9891354-3-6

All images are from the personal collection of the author. Use of images in this book is for historical and research purposes only, and is considered Fair Use. No infringement is intended or implied.

What are 'men's magazines'?

Just as the name implies, these were magazines for sale to the public which attempted to appeal to men. The vast majority of them did so with photographs of scantily-clad young women, while some employed thrilling short stories full of action and danger; many offered up non-fiction articles on interesting topics, news of the day, or – especially in the titles with titillating photos – were often about sexual topics. Humor, especially cartoons, was also a popular bit of content.

Just as with any medium that can easily identify its target audience, the men's magazines desperately sought to give their readers what they wanted, month after month (assuming the titles lasted that long) and keep them coming back. The women were voluptuous, the fiction was sensational, the covers were appealing: every effort was made, if time and budget allowed, for each issue to be as lurid and entertaining as possible, especially to the casual browser at the newsstand on the cusp of laying out his pocket change for an issue.

Unfortunately, many of the magazines in this volume fall way short of having the 'lurid' or 'entertaining' labels applied to them. Many publishers sprang up quickly, with the idea in mind of making a cheap, quick buck on this whole magazine racket – and after a month or three, their titles disappeared from the shelves. Many publications were poorly edited; their art direction was minimal, their photographs were lackluster, and sometimes material from previous issues or other sources was re-used. Some publishers thought so little of their product – or of their association with it – that they didn't even put their own names anywhere within. Or, they made up a new company name for a new title; if it was successful, they kept it, but if not, who cared? They scrapped it and moved on to the next one.

Why collect them?

The main reason to collect anything, of course, is because it's fun.

The men's magazines of the past are full of content that can still appeal to modern sensibilities. The women are, after all – despite the outdated hair styles and fuzzy black-and-white photography – still pleasant to look at for any red-blooded heterosexual male. The fiction is still lurid and exciting, even if a bit hard to swallow. And of course there is a distinct nostalgia factor at play when one looks at such things as the vintage advertising, the artwork, or the décor shown in the photographs. These magazines give us an idea of what life was like in the 1950's and 60's for men... or at least, what they *wanted* their lives to be like.

From the standpoint of collectibles, men's magazines are a largely untapped area. We live in a time when pretty much every comic book, every trading card, every coin or postage stamp has been extensively catalogued, photographed, and blogged about extensively. Price guides have taken much of the mystery out of many areas of collectibles, making even the rarest specimens known to the casual browser – but not in this area. Not yet! This book is hopefully a (pardon the phrase) pioneering work in the history of this collectibles category. Other books exist on the topic, but none this extensively (see the Bibliography a few pages forward).

What that means is that you, the reader of this book, have an opportunity to get in at the beginning. You have the chance to start collecting an item that hasn't yet been methodically catalogued and archived. While this volume isn't a price guide, what it does for the reader is to identify what's out there waiting to be collected. Most people think old *Playboy* issues are the beginning and end of this collectible category. Hardly! This book contains over 950 different titles listed. Many of them are fairly common, many difficult to find, and some are downright rare.

The best part of getting in on the ground floor of a new collectible, however, is the price. Since these magazines are still largely unknown to the larger collecting public, there is no agreed-upon pricing mechanism set up for individual issues or titles. Certainly, this can mean that sellers go overboard and price their items too high; it may also mean the interested buyer can swoop in and snag some great deals. If men's magazines become a widely-collected item, then those enthusiasts who moved in early and got their hands on the rarest and most sough-after items will be riding high. And the best part is, we don't yet know (beyond the apparance of Marilyn Monroe or Bettie Page on specific covers) which items those will be. This gives you, valued reader, as much chance of becoming a Top Collector as anyone else.

What different types of men's magazines are there?

The primary type, comprising perhaps 75-80% of the total, is the **girlie magazine**. It is so called because its primary purpose is to deliver photographs of semi-nude and (later) nude women. In the early 1950's nearly all of the women photographed had their nipples covered; the most a man could hope for was a hint through a see-through nightie, or the curve of an unclothed buttock. Gradually, however, both breasts and buttocks were allowed to be revealed; pubic hair wouldn't be shown until the late 1960's. Before that, objects were strategically photographed to cover the models' pudenda, or they wore panties, or always had one leg covering the offending area. This is contrary to popular notions about such magazines by people who are ignorant of them. These might also be called **nudie magazines** or **stag magazines**.

Glamor magazines were a subset of the girlie mags, and might feature either fully-clothed or semi-nude models, but the emphasis in these was always on very tasteful, professionally photographed women in upscale settings.

The **adventure fiction** magazines contained fiction that appealed to men – usually stories set in faraway places, featuring a rugged protagonist who succeeded against great odds. During the 1950's, many ex-soldiers felt a twinge of nostalgia for the far-flung adventures they had experienced during World War II; but, saddled with a wife, kids, and a mortgage, the most they could hope for was to read about such things in their favorite periodicals.

The **slicks**, also known as the **male sophisticates**, sought to appeal to a more upscale readership – or at least, appear to do so. *Playboy* was certainly the model of this type of magazine, offering a mixture of fiction, non-fiction, tasteful pictorials, and cartoons, but covered with a veneer of respectability and cultural sophistication... or at least, sophistication as it might have appeared within the aspirations of college guys who longed to graduate and get a job in the big city, as well as an apartment where they could throw cocktail parties with swanky chicks. The emphasis on these was always to hold out a promise of a more appealing lifestyle to the average joe, and to advise him on how to handle such a lifestyle should he ever luck into it.

Cartoon and humor magazines were pretty much what one might expect, but for the purposes of this book, only those titles which often also featured photos of attractive young women – and many did – are included.

The **popular digests** of (primarily) the 1950's offered readers news, scandals, and celebrity gossip all in a very portable and inexpensive package. Only a few titles, however, also featured pictures of lovely young ladies, and it is those which are included here.

Photography and figure-study magazines were found to be a sure-fire way to dodge local obscenity laws in the 1940's and early 50's. After all, if nudity could be found among the great works of art throughout history, how could it be denied to modern male patrons? Thus many titles rose up which were little more than excuses to show nude or nearly-nude women. Often they were a bit obvious in their ruse and were busted anyway.

Nudist mags were put out by organizations which honestly and sincerely pushed nudism as an alternative lifestyle choice. Often these were available only to persons within the nudist community. In any case, men who sought diligently to get their hands on such titles for their prurient value were usually disappointed. Not only did they not feature much in the way of buxom young women, but very often the front genitals were airbrushed out of photos. Most of the images dealt with dumpy housewives or their gravity-challenged husbands anyway; and yes, many of the nudist mags contained children. But for erotic value, modern readers (as they were in the past) are likely to be crestfallen when they actually open one of these periodicals for the first time. (The fiction contained in some of these titles is hilarious, however.)

Which titles are included in this book? Which ones aren't?

The magazines included in this volume were all legally available for sale on American newsstands or behind counters in various types of retail outlets. They all had a cover price and featured issues which were dated between January 1950 and December 1969 – that is, titles which began before or continued after these dates are included, as long as they had issues that fall within this time frame.

There are a number of titles that are excluded for various reasons, however. Specialty fetish magazines, for example, are largely not covered, since many of these were not cover priced or sold at normal outlets.

Magazines for swinger hook-ups are not included, since they mainly consisted of non-pictorial material.

Magazines devoted to pornographic photography (that is, with overt sexual depictions over and above simple nudity) are not included. This is largely not a problem since this material really didn't start to appear in America before 1968. Some of the titles included, however, may have featured more pornographic material if they lasted into the 1970's; but they had to have at least a few nude-only issues for inclusion.

Likewise, titles devoted to softcore or hardcore films, whether giving reviews or offering photo stills, are not included.

'Pulp' magazines that survived into the 1950's, although many of them contained fiction aimed at a male audience, are not included.

Magazines that concentrated on female celebrities, even though they might have fallen into the 'non-nude glamor' category, are not included.

Nudist magazines are not covered, but may be dealt with in a future publication.

Homosexual titles – which have traditionally been unavailable through normal channels anyway – are not included.

Sports magazines, which one might think would appeal to men during this time period, generally do not fall within the purview of this book, although some of the titles given here might contain fiction or articles centered around certain sports or athletes. Big-game hunting was certainly a common theme in many fiction stories due to the appeal of man-vs.-nature tales.

Amateur and small-press titles are not included.

The Whitestone Publications titles, which are more akin to magazine-sized booklets, as well as the Fawcett how-to magazine-sized booklets, are not included.

A few titles may have slipped through the cracks, including the 1950's digests, as well as earlier photography/figure study magazines.

Why 1950 – 1969?

This period was certainly the Golden Age of men's magazines, with (as you will find in this book) literally hundreds of different titles being available. As with American comic books, there was far more variety and imaginative content available during this period than before or, sadly, after. This era saw the debut of the unclothed female breast as well as, eventually, the rest of the female form.

But the main reason is simply that before about 1952, the modern 'men's magazine' as we know it did not exist. And by the early 1970's, the men's fiction magazines were largely gone, while hardcore pornography slowly usurped everything else. 1950 to 1969 represents an even 20 years, and that's a good enough time frame for this book to cover.

Notes on a few prominent publishers

The company referred to as Atlas in this volume is known under several different names, but here it just refers to the various publishing enterprises of Martin Goodman. Goodman was involved in several aspects of the publishing industry from the 1930's to the late 1960's. Goodman published pulp magazines (such as *Mystery Tales* and *Marvel Science Stories*), paperback books (under the Lion imprint) and, starting in 1939, comic books. It was the comic books that really took off, but not until the mid-1960's, because Goodman's comic publishing arm became what is now known as Marvel Comics. For the purposes of this volume, however, Goodman's importance lies mainly in his adventure-fiction titles (largely under the Magazine Management imprint) and his cartoon titles (the Humorama line).

American Art Agency was the company founded by Milton Luros during the 1950's, at first as an agency to find work for Luros and his fellow artists in New York. Luros moved his family and the company out to California later that decade, where he became art director for Knight Publishing, which put out the titles *Knight* and *Adam*. Studying their method, he put out his own title, *Cocktail*, the following year; it was sold exclusively in liquor stores, but was enough of a hit for his American Art Agency to become a full-fledged publisher. Luros soon began his own distribution company, Parliament News, and it is under the 'Parliament' name that many of his publications are remembered. For the next two decades Parliament books were known for their high-quality photography and top-shelf production values.

Myron Fass, mentioned a few times in this volume, was a publisher of quick-and-dirty titles whose only concern was selling magazines, no matter how lurid or offensive the subject matter. The comic magazines printed under his Eerie Publcations banner were some of the bloodiest and goriest images ever to appear on newsstands. He was first to the stands with a magazine devoted to the just-deceased Elvis Presley. He had titles devoted to UFO's, gangsters, psychic powers, sci-fi fandom, crime, and – pertinent to this volume – he also did such girlie mag titles as *Buccaneer*, *Jaguar*, and *Bold*.

Bibliography

Bad Mags I & II, Tom Brinkmann. Headpress, 2008-2009.

Cult Magazine Checklist Guide, Alan Betrock. Shake Books, 2000.

Cult Magazines A to Z, edited by Earl Kemp and Luis Ortiz. Nonstop Press, 2009.

Dian Hanson's The History of Men's Magazines, edited by Dian Hanson. Taschen, 2005 (4 volumes).

Illustrated History of Girlie Magazines, Mark Gabor. Harmony Books, 1984.

It's A Man's World, Adam Parfrey. Feral House, 2003.

Men's (Girlie) Magazines Price & Identification Guide, Jack C. Denison. TICN, 1994.

Men's Adventure Magazines, edited by Jim Heimann and Nina Wiener. Taschen, 2008.

Pin-Up Mania!, Alan Betrock. Shake Books, 1993.

The author wishes to express a great debt to Phil Stephensen-Payne, whose magazine indexing website at www.philsp.com was an absolutely indispensible source of information. In fact, this book could not have been possible without it.

3-D Girls

'A man's magazine with dimension.'

M.M. Publishing, New York NY.

1965. One-shot.

Pictorials.

This magazine presented anaglyph 3-D photos of semi-nude women. It came with red-and-green 3-D glasses attached.

3-D Pinups

Models Publishing Co., New York NY.

1953. One-shot.

Pictorials.

Came with red-and-green anaglyph 3-D glasses attached.

21

Monogram Publications, Los Angeles CA.

1955 – 1960? ~20 issues, with at least one Annual.

Nonfiction, pictorials.

21

American Art Agency Inc., Hollywood CA (Parliament).

1968 – 1973? ~8 issues?

Apparently not related to the previous Monogram title, this magazine may have started with its first issue designated v.2, #1.

38/26/34

American Art Agency Inc., Hollywood CA (Parliament).

Late 1960's – 1983? How many issues were produced?

Pictorials.

There was also at least 1 calendar produced, for 1974.

711

Universe Publications Inc.

March 1960 – ? More than 1 issue produced?

1,001 Nights

1965. More than 1 issue produced?

Ace

Four Star Publications, New York NY.

Oct 1957 – 1980's. 100+ issues, including Annuals.

Fiction, nonfiction, pictorials.

The first two issues (June and August, 1957) were actually *Sport Adventure*. The first real issue of *Ace* is v.1 #3.

A few of the annuals are titled *Ace High*.

3-D Girls

21 (Monogram)

21 (Parliament)

38/26/34

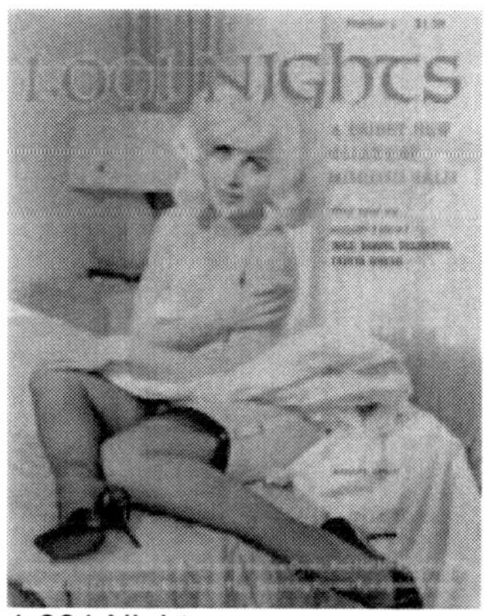

1,001 Nights

Ace

Ace

Ace

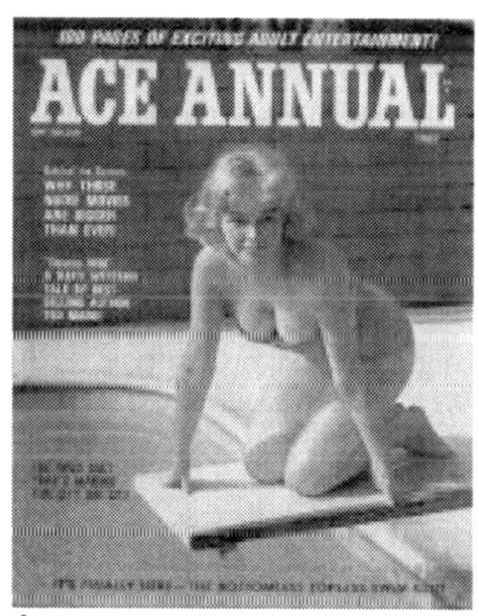

Ace

Action

'The best in lusty adventure.'

Picture Magazines, Inc. 6 issues.

March – December 1953.

Adventure fiction, nonfiction.

Did this turn into a girlie title for an issue or two?

Action For Men

Vista Publications (Atlas-Diamond).

March 1958? – 1978? 100+ issues.

Fiction, nonfiction, black-and-white pictorials.

May have originated with *Real Action For Men* in 1957.

Action Illustrated

Major Magazines Corp., Sparta IL.

1962 – 1963. 5 issues?

Adventure fiction.

Action Life

Atlas.

August 1963 – November 1964. 6 issues.

Adventure fiction.

Adam

Knight Publishing Corp., Los Angeles CA.

January 1952 – 1996? 100+ issues plus Annuals.

Pictorials, fiction, nonfiction.

This was one one of the longest-running and greatest of the vintage men's magazines; thankfully, most surviving issues are today not too difficult or expensive to find.

Note: there were several other different titles published as part of the *Adam* family, some of which we cover in separate entries. The only one we don't cover, because this collection excludes film mags, is *Adam Film World*.

In addition to the magazines and calendars, there were also at least 6 record albums published using the *Adam* name, under the title *Adam Stag Party Special*.

Adam Bedside Reader

Knight Publishing Corp., Los Angeles CA.

1959 – 1972. 54 issues.

Nonfiction, fiction, pictorials.

Adam Calendar

Knight Publishing Corp., Los Angeles CA.

1959 – 1974? 15 issues?

Pictorials.

Action

Action For Men

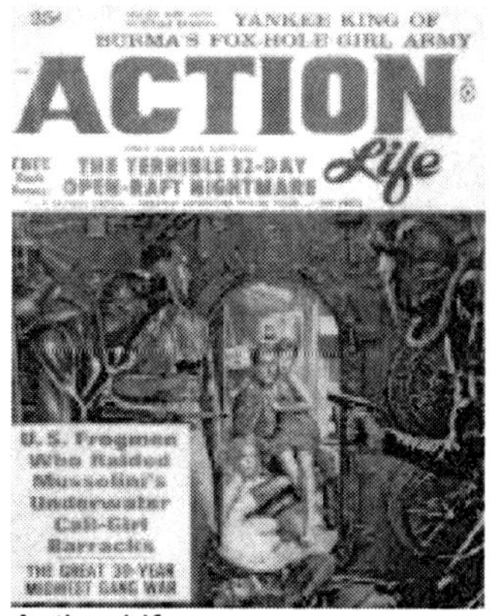

Action Life

Adam

Adam

Adam

Adam Bedside Reader

Adam Bedside Reader

Adam Calendar

Adam Sextra Laughs

Knight Publishing Corp., Los Angeles CA.

1968 – 1973? 10 issues published?

Cartoons, pictorials.

Adam Special Report

Knight Publishing Corp., Los Angeles CA.

1969 – 1972? At least 9 issues published.

Nonfiction.

Adam Stag Humor

Knight Publishing Corp., Los Angeles CA.

1964 – 1969? At least 5 issues published.

Cartoons.

Adventure

Popular Publications.

November 1910 – 1971? 800+ issues.

Adventure fiction.

This was a pulp fiction that lasted into the early 70's. During the men's magazine heyday, it fit right in with the other publications offering this type of entertainment.

Adventure For Men

Jalart House, New York NY.

October 1965 – Summer 1974. ~40 issues, including at least 2 Yearbooks.

Adventure fiction.

Adventure Life

Atlas/Vista Pub.

January 1957 – March 1959; August 1961 – May 1963. 19 issues? (possibly 18)

Fiction.

This was a fiction magazine, published in two different series (the August 1961 restarts with v.1, #1), both by Atlas (Vista Publications being an imprint of Atlas).

Adventure Trails

Atlas.

January 1957. One-shot.

Adventure fiction.

Adventures For Men

Sterling Group, New York NY.

July – October 1959. 4 issues.

Fiction.

This was a brief retitling of *Man's Illustrated* for only four issues, which continued again afterward with the original title.

Adam Sextra Laughs

Adam Special Report

Adam Stag Humor

Adventure

Adventure

Adventure For Men

Adventure Life

Adventure Trails

Adventures For Men

Affair

American Art Agency Inc., Hollywood CA (Parliament).

1963 – 1978? ~50 issues?

Pictorials.

This was another Parliament magazine with an odd publishing schedule., which may have skipped a few years between certain issues.

After Dark

After Dark Pub., Union City NJ.

December 1959 – ? How many issues?

Pictorials, nonfiction, cartoons.

After Dark

American Art Agency Inc., Hollywood CA (Parliament).

Early 1960's. More than 1 issue published?

Pictorials.

After Hours

Jay Publishing, Philadelphia PA.

1957. 4 issues.

Nonfiction plus articles.

This was the first magazine published by James Warren, whose later Warren Publishing would gain fame for such titles as *Famous Monsters of Filmland* and *Vampirella*.

Bettie Page appeared in more than one issue.

After Hours

Comet Publications, Los Angeles CA; Manafest Publications, Los Alamitos CA.

1963 – 1968? How many issues published?

Pictorials.

Was there a third magazine from this era with the same title?

All Man

Stanley Publications, New York NY.

March 1959 – 1980? 100+ issues, including at least 5 larger Special/Quarterly issues.

Fiction and nonfiction plus pictorials.

This was primarily a men's adventure fiction magazine until the July 1967 issue (v.8 #1), where it became a girlie pictorial magazine with photo covers.

Amateur Art and Camera

Camerarts Publishing Co., Chicago IL.

1950 – 1959. 50+ issues.

Pictorials.

Affair

After Dark

After Dark (Parliament)

After Hours (Jay)

After Hours (Comet)

All Man

All Man

All Man

Amateur Art & Camera

Amateur Screen and Photography
Camerarts Publishing Co., Chicago IL.
1950 - 1958. 50+ issues published.
Pictorials.
Becomes *Figure Art* in 1959.

American Beauties
Capitol Stories Inc., Derby CT (Charlton).
Black and white interiors. Measures 9 by 12 inches.
November 1952 – Fall 1953. 4 issues.
Pictorials.

American Man
'The exciting magazine of thrilling adventure.'
Popular Library Pub.
May 1965 – May 1966? 4 issues?
Fiction.

American Manhood
'The virile magazine.'
Weider Publications, Jersey City NJ.
January – July 1953. 6 issues.
Adventure fiction.
For notes, see *Mr. America*.

American Scene
See **Scene**.

Angel
1960's. At least 2 issues.
Pictorials.

Animal Life
Weider Publications, Jersey City NJ.
December 1953 – June 1955. 8 issues.
Fiction, particularly man vs. animal.
This title became *Safari* with the August (or July?) 1955 issue.

A-OK For Men
Jalart House, New York NY.
October 1962 – October/November 1963. 5 issues.
Adventure fiction.

Amateur Screen & Photog

American Beauties

American Manhood

Angel

Animal Life

Animal Life

A-OK For Men

A-OK For Men

A-OK For Men

Argosy

Popular Publications.

September 1943 – November/December 1979. 100+ issues.

Fiction, nonfiction.

Argosy had actually started as far back as 1882, and went through various formats. Sept. 1943 was the first regular-sized, 'slick' magazine issue, and it maintained this version through the end of the 70's.

Art and Camera

See *Amateur Art and Camera*.

Art Photography

Titan Publications, Chicago IL.

1949 - 1957. ~100 issues.

Pictorials.

Babe

American Art Agency Inc., Hollywood CA (Parliament).

1960's. At least 4 issues.

Pictorials.

Babes and Dolls

Acme.

Late 1960's – early 70's? At least 3 issues.

Pictorials.

Baby Doll

Sari Publishing Co., North Hollywood CA; Rilgac Publishing Co., Hollywood CA.

Early 1960's. At least 3 issues.

Bachelor

Atlas; Magtab Publishing, New York NY.

September 1956 – November 1958; March 1961 – 1983? 100+ issues, including several annuals between 1957 and 1981.

Pictorials, fiction, nonfiction.

The first version of this magazine was published by Atlas through 1958; it was apparently purchased by Magtab who began publishing it in March 1961, continuing the numbering from *Men in Adventure* for some reason.

Bachelor Party

American Art Agency Inc., Hollywood CA (Parliament).

1968 – early 1970's. ~10 issues published?

Pictorials.

Argosy

Argosy

Art Photography

Babes and Dolls

Baby Doll

Bachelor

Bachelor

Bachelor

Bachelor Party

Backstage Follies

November 1956 – October 1957? 5 issues?

Pictorials and cartoons.

Bare

'The naked truth.'

D. & L. Publishing Co., Los Angeles CA.

April 1953 – 1960? 50+ issues.

Black and white interiors. Measures 4.5 by 6.5 inches.

Nonfiction, pictorials.

The November 1954 issue features Bettie Page on the cover, and thus sells for a lot more than other issues.

Bare (Exposes)

Measures 5.5 by 8.5 inches.

1959 – 1960. 4 issues published?

Pictorials, nonfiction, fiction.

This title was more a traditional girlie magazine for its first two issues, and featured *Bare* on the cover; the last two issues were called *Bare Exposes* and offered scandal stories as well as pinup photos.

Bare (3rd)

Spring 1964. More than 1 issue?

The Bare Breast Rebellion

Sari Publishing Co., North Hollywood CA.

Black and white interior, with color centerfold.

1966. One-shot.

Nonfiction, pictorials.

This magazine was actually a comprehensive listing of California's topless bars, with plenty of relevant information (such as the names of prominent performers) and illustrated with a large number of black-and-white photos.

Battle Attack

Actual Publishing Co., New York NY.

March – July 1957. 3 issues.

War fiction.

Battle Cry

Stanley Publications, New York NY.

December 1955 – 1972? 100+ issues.

War fiction.

The numbering continues from a previous comic book by the same publisher, so that the first issue is v.1 #21.

Backstage Follies

Bare (1st)

Bare (1st)

Bare (1st)

Battle Attack

Battle Attack

Battle Cry

Battle Cry

Battle Cry

Battle Station

Action Publishing Co.

November 1961. Only issue?

War fiction.

Battlefield

Newsstand Publications, New York NY (Atlas).

February 1957 – November 1959. 9 issues.

War fiction; pictorials also?

Beau (2nd)

1962. More than 1 issue produced?

Beau

Publishers Development Corp., London, England.

June 1966 – July 1968? 25 issues?

Pictorials and nonfiction.

This was a British publication distributed within the U.S. This was sort of the British equivalent of *Modern Man*.

Beau Femme

1965 – 1966? At least 6 issues.

Beauties

Black and white interior.

1950 – 1951. 2 issues.

Pictorials.

Beautiful Girls

Beautiful Publications, New York NY.

Black and white interior. Measures 8 by 10.5 inches.

October 1950 – March 1951. 2 issues.

Pictorials.

Beauty Bazaar

American Art Agency Inc.; Windsor Publishing Co., Hollywood CA (Parliament).

1963 – 1972? ~15 issues?

Pictorials.

This is one of those Parliament publications that started out showing semi-nude women, eventually going further toward outright pornography; although it was supposed to come out four times a year, it took several years to get through at least Volume 4.

Battlefield

Battlefield

Beau (1962)

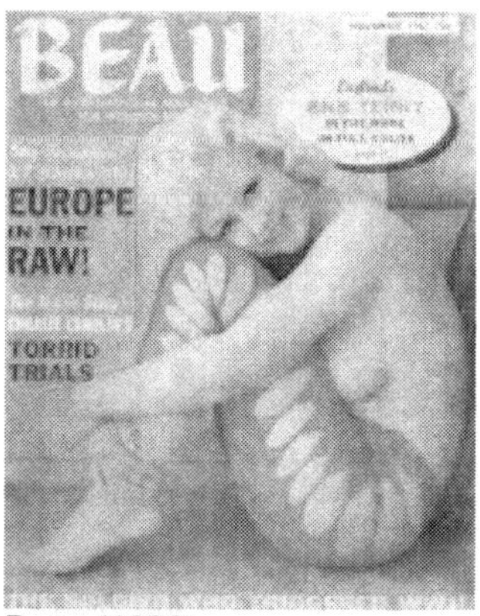

Beau (1966)

Beau (1966)

Beau Femme

Beauties

Beautiful Girls

Beauty Bazaar

Beauty Parade

Beauty Parade Inc., New York NY.

Black and white interior.

October 1941 – February 1956. 86 issues.

Pictorials, nonfiction.

This was one of the 'classic' good-girlie magazines that couldn't quite hang in there once competition started getting more intense.

Beauty Photography

Male Magazines Inc., New York NY (Atlas).

1957. One-shot.

Pictorials.

Bedside

1957 – 1958? 2 issues published?

Cartoons, pictorials, fiction, nonfiction.

Bedside Banquet

1960's. More than 1 issue produced?

Belles

Triumph News Co. Inc., Van Nuys CA.

1960's. More than 2 issues?

Pictorials.

Best For Men

Best For Men Publications.

June 1961 – January 1980. 87 issues.

Pictorials.

Note: Issue #4 is easily found and was almost certainly a warehouse find.

Between Us

Black and white interiors. Oversized magazine.

December 1949 – October 1950? At least 6 issues.

Nonfiction, pictorials.

Bewitch

Comet Publications, Los Angeles CA.

1960's. At least 4 issues?

Bewitched

Comet Publications, Los Angeles CA.

1960's. How many issues were published?

Is this a continution of the previous title?

Beauty Parade

Beauty Parade

Beauty Photography

Bedside Banquet

Belles

Best For Men

Between Us

Bewitch

Bewitched

Big & Bouncy
World Wide News Co., Cleveland OH.
Black and white interiors, with color centerfolds. Measures 6 by 9 inches.
1960's. At least 2 regular issues, plus at least 1 Annual.
Pictorials.

Big Adventure
Matclif Publications, New York NY.
September 1960 – June 1961. 5 issues.
Adventure fiction.

Big Time
Art Enterprises Inc., Los Angeles CA.
Measures 11 by 17 inches.
June – August 1949; January – July 1951. 7 issues.
Pictorials, nonfiction.
This magazine changed its name to *Taboo* between October 1949 and December 1950.

Bikini
Black and white interior, with color centerfold.
1963. Only 1 issue?
Pictorials.

Black Garter
Synmag Publishing.
Early 1960's? At least 3 issues produced.
Pictorials.

Black Hose
Dominion Publishing Co., North Hollywood CA.
Late 1960's – early 1970's. At least 15 issues published.
Pictorials, nonfiction.
Was there more than one magazine under this title?

Black Lace
Rilgac Publishing Co., Hollywood CA.
1961 – 1963? At least 6 issues.
Pictorials.

Black Lace (2nd)
Late 1960's? More than 1 issue produced?

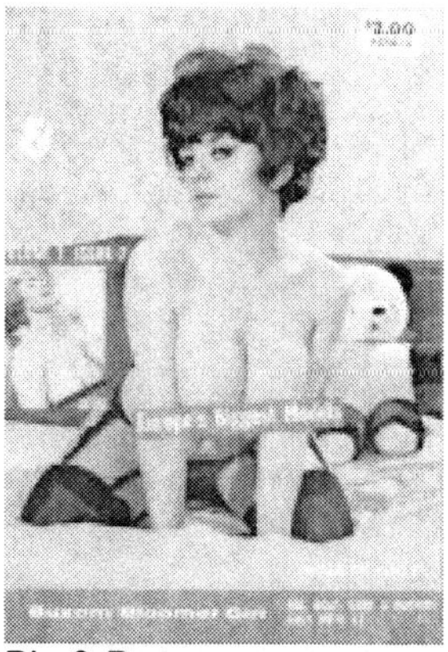

Big & Bouncy

Big Adventure

Big Time

Bikini

Black Garter

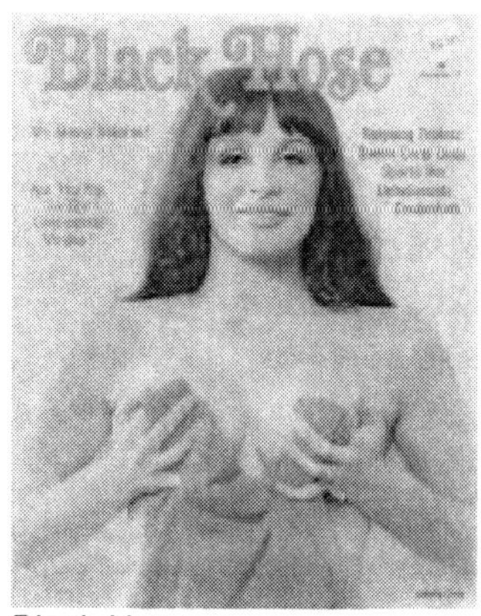

Black Hose

Black Lace (Rilgac)

Black Lace (Rilgac)

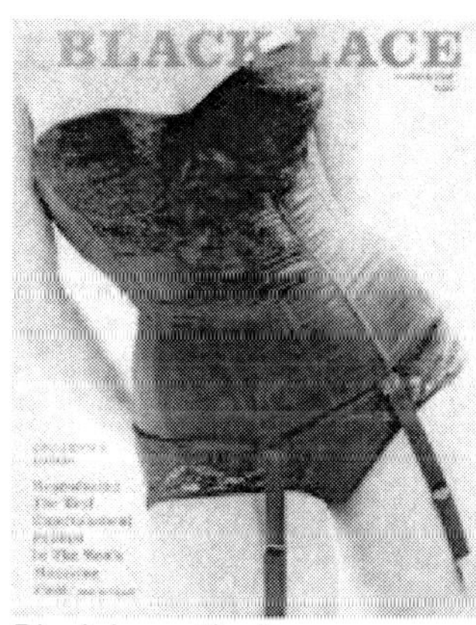

Black Lace (2nd)

Black Magic

American Art Agency Inc., Hollywood CA (Parliament).

Black and white, and color photos.

1963 – 1971? ~30 issues?

Pictorials, nonfiction, fiction.

This was another Parliament publication whose content was at least 80% (semi-) nude photos, devolving into full 'beaver shot' nude photography by the 70's.

Black n Blue

1960's. More than 1 issue produced?

Black Nylons

Sampson Publishing and Distribution Co., New York NY.

March 1962 – 1967. At least 10 issues produced.

Bettie Page appears on the cover of v.2 #2.

Black Nylons

World Wide News Co., Cleveland OH.

Black and white interiors, color centerfolds. Measures 6 by 9 inches.

1966 – 1967? At least 6 issues?

Pictorials.

Black Orchids

Health Knowledge Inc., New York NY.

Late 1960's. At least 5 issues published.

Pictorials.

Focused on African-American models.

Black Satin

Sampson Publishing and Distribution Co., New York NY.

September 1962 – October 1963. At least 7 issues produced.

Were there two issues numbered v.1 #4?

Black Silk Stockings

Batters Publications Inc., Hollywood CA.

1958-1961. 18 issues, plus 1 Annual.

Pictorials.

Black Silk Stockings

Period Publishing.

1962 – 1969. ~30 issues.

Pictorials.

Black Magic

Black Magic

Black n Blue

Black Nylons (Sampson)

Black Nylons (WWN)

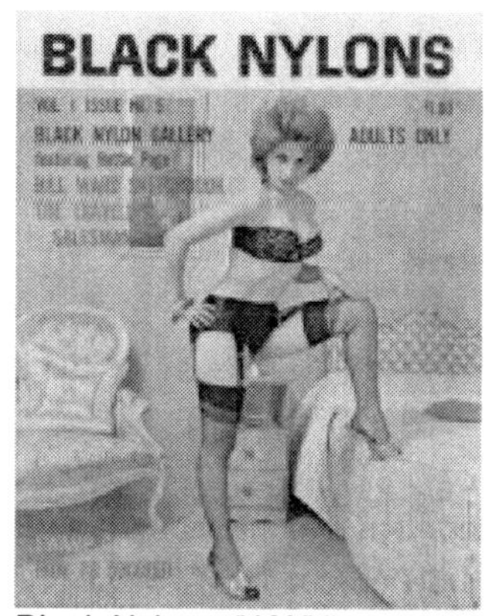

Black Nylons (WWN)

Black Satin

Black Silk Stockings (1958)

Black Silk Stockings (1962)

Black Stocking Parade
Connoisseur Publications.
Black and white interiors. Measures 6 by 9 inches.
1962 – 1963. 6 issues?
Pictorials.

Black Velvet
Orly Publishing Co., New York NY.
1960 – 1961. 4 issues?

Black Velvet
Tuxedo Books.
1963. More than 1 issue produced?

Blast
Sari Publishing Co., North Hollywood CA.
1961 – 1966? How many issues published?
Pictorials, nonfiction.

Blaze
Art Enterprises Inc., Los Angeles CA.
1961 – 1963. 7 issues?
Pictorials.

Blondes Brunettes Redheads
ABC Publications, El Monte CA;Tri-S Publications, Hollywood CA.
Black and white interiors.
1959 – 1964. At least 6 issues.
Issue #3 has the same basic cover as *Sizzle* #8.

Blue Mist
Early 1960's. How many issues published?
Pictorials.

Bluebook (For Men)
H.S. Publications / Hanro Corp. / QMG Magazine Corp.
October 1960 – May 1975. 109 issues, plus 2 Annuals.
Fiction, nonfiction.
A successor to the original long-running *Bluebook* magazine, for the purposes of this book this title began in 1960 with v.100, issue #1, lasting through mid-1975.

Black Stocking Parade

Black Velvet (1963)

Blast

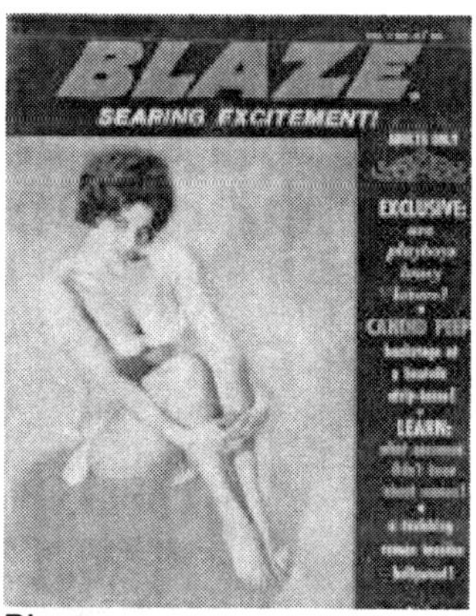

Blaze

Blondes Brunettes etc.

Blue Mist

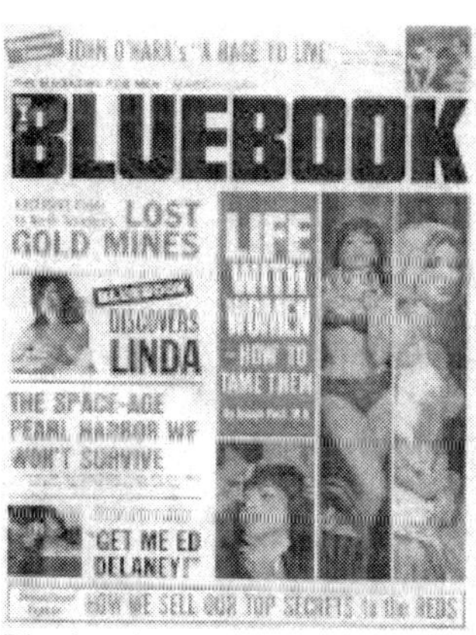

Bluebook

Bluebook

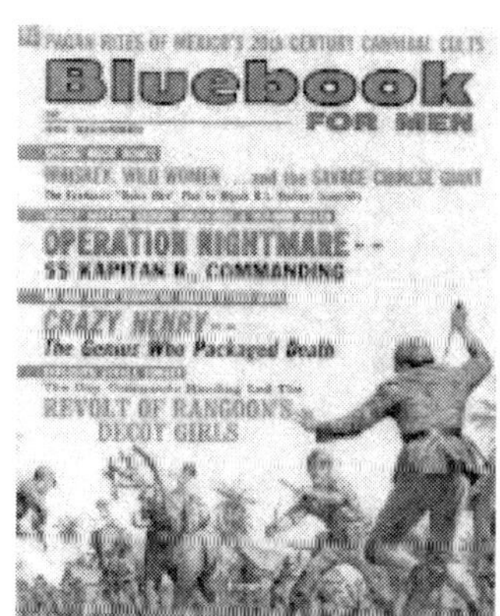

Bluebook

Blush

Orly Publications, New York NY.

1962. Only 1 issue produced?

Nonfiction, pictorials.

Apparently all of the material in this title was produced by women.

Body Shop

American Art Agency Inc., Hollywood CA (Parliament).

1963 – 1969. 24 issues?

Pictorials.

Bold

'The pocket magazine for men.'

Pocket Magazines Inc., Atlanta GA; Publication Management Corp., Atlanta GA.

Black and white interiors. Measures 4 by 6 inches.

1954 – 1963? 80+ issues?

Nonfiction, pictorials.

The March 1955 issue has a great Bettie Page cover and is thus more expensive than others.

Bold

1968 – 1974. 30+ issues, including at least one 'Best Of' larger-sized issue.

Pictorials, nonfiction.

Bold Girls!

Black and white interiors, with color centerfolds.

1950's – early 60's. How many issues?

Bettie Page appeared on the cover of v.2 #1.

Bold Men

Cape Magazine Management Corp., New York NY.

Black and white interiors.

December 1960 – September 1961. 4 issues.

Nonfiction, pictorials.

This was a quick-and-dirty little publication that wasn't afraid to pile on the sleaze. In fact, the image of the Bedouin warrior on the December 1960 cover was stolen from the May 1959 cover of *Savage* (which they also published, but still).

Bombshells of Burlesque

Selbee Associates Inc., New York NY.

Black and white interiors.

1950's. At least 4 issues.

Bon-Bon

1960's. How many issues were produced?

Blush

Body Shop

Bold (1954)

Bold (1954)

Bold (1968)

Bold Girls

Bold Men

Bombshells of Burlesque

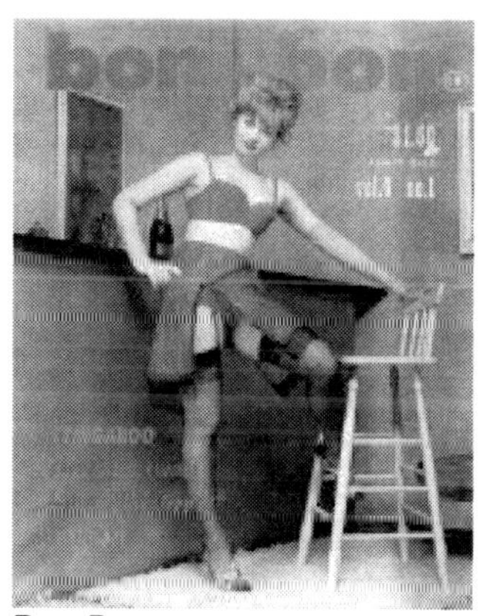
Bon-Bon

Boudoir
Black and white interiors, color centerfold.
1960 – 1961? 5+ issues.
Nonfiction, pictorials, cartoons.

Bounce
1960's. How many issues published?

Bouncy Babes
Health Knowledge Inc., New York NY.
Late 1960's. At least 4 issues.
Pictorials.

Bounder
Art Enterprises Inc., Los Angeles CA.
1962. 3 regular issues plus 1 Annual.
Pictorials, nonfiction.

Bra Busters
Sampson Publishing and Distribution Co., New York NY.
1960. More than 1 issue published?
Not to be confused with the later magazine which started in the 1970's.

Brave
Cape Magazine Management Inc., New York NY.
November 1956 – September 1958. 5 issues.
Adventure fiction.
Became *Savage Adventures For Men*.

Bravo
1959. More than 1 issue published?

Breezy
Humorama Inc., New York NY (Atlas).
Black and white interiors. Measures 5.5 by 7.5 inches.
February 1954 – 1959; 1967 – 1972? 65+ issues?
Cartoons, pictorials.
Apparently this magazine started back up again in the late 1960's after having been cancelled for several years.

Boudoir

Boudoir

Bounce

Bounder

Bounder

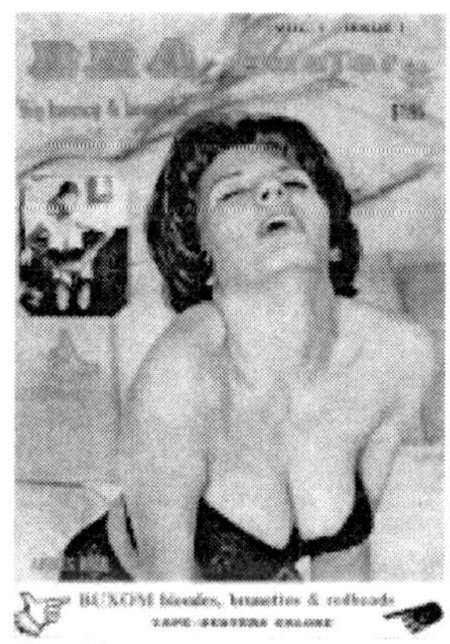

Bra Busters

Bouncy Babes

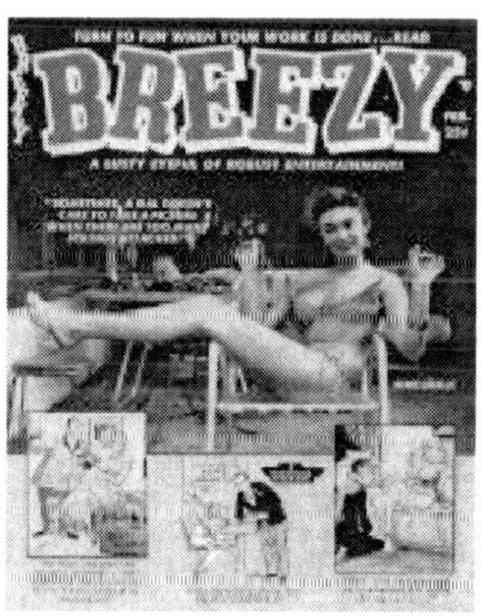

Breezy

Breezy

Brief
Mutual Magazine Corp. (Atlas).
Black and white interiors.
December 1952 – October 1956. 24 issues.
Nonfiction, pictorials.

Brigade
Flightplan Inc., New York NY.
Black-and-white interior.
October 1962 – May 1963? 4 issues?
Fiction, nonfiction, pictorials.
This was another quick-and-dirty magazine that appeared for only a brief time.

Broad Tales
Dominion Publishing Co., North Hollywood CA; Triumph News Co. Inc., Van Nuys CA.
1969. At least 4 issues.
Pictorials.

Broad Views
Press Arts Inc., Canoga Park CA.
1965 – 1970? At least 23 issues, plus an Annual for 1965.
Pictorials.

Broadside
American Art Agency Inc., Hollywood CA (Parliament).
1964 – early 1970's? 20+ issues.
Pictorials.

Bronze Beauties (Revue)
Press Arts Inc., Canoga Park CA.
1965 – 1970's? How many issues published?
Pictorials.
As one can imagine, this title concentrated on non-Caucasian models.
This magazine must have continued at least until 1975, as a calendar for that year exists under this title.

Brunette
Brunette Publications, Los Angeles CA.
1961 – 1963. ~5 issues?
Pictorials.

Bubbles
Early 1960's. How many issues were published?

Brief

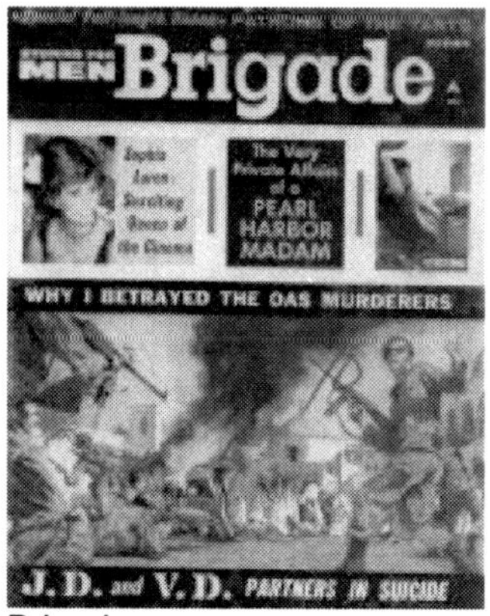

Brigade

Broad Tales

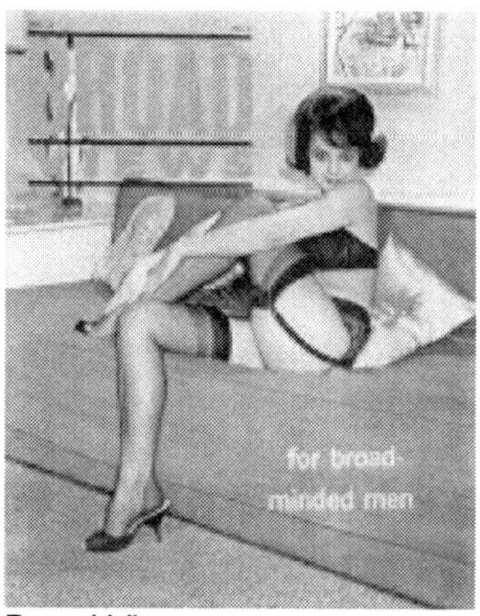

Broad Views

Broadside

Broadside

Bronze Beauties

Brunette

Bubbles

Buccaneer

Press Arts Inc., Canoga Park CA; Tempest Publications, New York NY.

1968 – 1970? 10 issues?

Pictorials.

Busty

Press Arts Inc., Canoga Park CA.

Black and white interior with color centerfold.

1960's. 40+ issues?

Pictorials.

Cabaret

Titan Publications, Chicago IL.

March 1955 – September 1957. 31 issues plus at least one larger Special Issue.

Nonfiction, pictorials.

This magazine catered to its readership by focusing on burlesque, strippers, glamour photography, etc.

Note: The March and May 1955 issues are nearly identical, although the dates of each are clearly given on the covers.

Cabaret Queens

Titan Publications, Chicago IL.

1955 – 1976. 50 issues.

Nonfiction, pictorials.

This was a larger-sized version of *Cabaret* that was released irregularly over the years. By the late 60's, however, it started to hold to a regular quarterly schedule.

Also known as *Cabaret Quarterly* and *Cabaret Yearbook.*

Cad

CAD Publishing Co., New York NY.

June 1965 – September 1970. 22 regular issues plus 2 larger 'Banner' editions.

Nonfiction, pictorials.

Cad was the usual general-interest men's magazine was semi-nude pictorials, articles of self-help or topical interest, film reviews, etc. Infrequently published, it's not among the top such titles of the era, but is still a fun read.

Note: the February 1968 issue was cover-titled *Cad Spectacular*, the June and September 1968 issues were *Cad Bizarre*.

Note also that three *Cad* 'Banner Editions' apparently exist (#1 being the most common by far); these are simply unsold overruns bound together with a new cover. They are not included in the issue total above.

Buccaneer

Busty

Cabaret

Cabaret

Cabaret

Cabaret Queens

Cad

Cad

Cad

Camera Art

Camerarts Publishing Co., Chicago IL.

1957 – 1960. 12 regular issues plus 1 Annual.

Pictorials, nonfiction.

Note that the 1957 and 1960 issues were released and numbered separately under the title *Camera Arts Illustrated*; the remainder all came out in 1959.

Campus Dolls

Bruce-Royal Publishing, Derby CT.

1964 – 1965? At least 2 issues published, possibly more.

Candid

Manly Publications Inc., New York NY.

September 1953 – May 1954. 4 issues.

Nonfiction, pictorials.

Candid

Sari Publishing Co., North Hollywood CA.

September 1958 – 1979? 100+ issues published, including larger special issues.

Pictorials.

This title had a rather erratic publishing schedule during its history, with some years producing only a few issues, while the 1970's saw it as a monthly title.

Candid Pinups

1956 – 1959. 13 issues produced?

Pictorials.

Candid Reader

Sari Publishing Co., North Hollywood CA.

1960 – 1963. Apparently 5 issues were produced.

This was an offshoot of Sari's *Candid* magazine.

Candid Whirl

Actual Publishing Co.

July 1952 – June 1953. 5 issues.

Pictorials, nonfiction.

Candida

Tower Publications.

1958 – 1963? At least 6 issues known.

Pictorials.

This was a title change from *Sex & Censorship*, starting with the third issue.

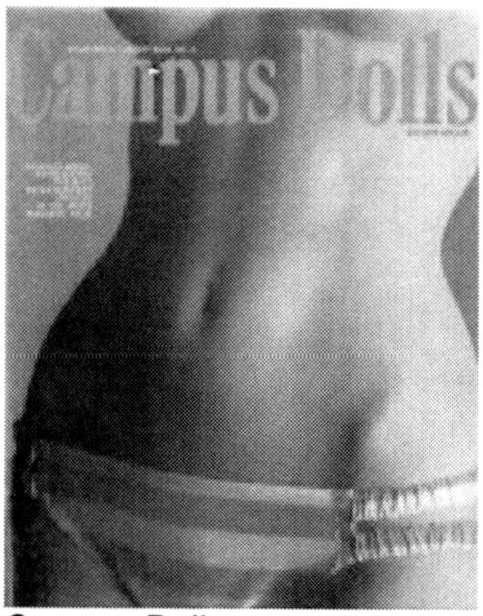
Campus Dolls

Candid (1953)

Candid

Candid

Candid

Candid Pinups

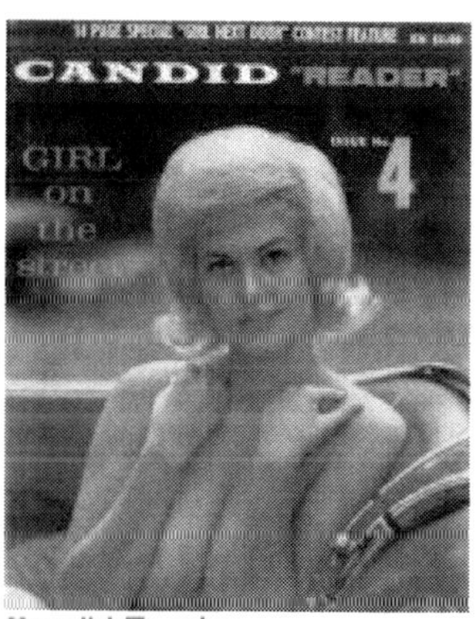

Candid Reader

Candid Whirl

Candida

Candlelight

American Art Agency Inc., Hollywood CA (Parliament).

Black and white, and color photos.

1964 – 1965? At least 4 issues.

Pictorials.

Caper

Dee Publishing Co., Los Angeles CA; See Magazines Inc.

October 1956 – 1983? 100+ issues plus several Annual/omnibus issues.

Fiction, nonfiction, and pictorials.

The Annuals, which ranged from 1959 to the mid-1970's, went by such names as *Caper's Treasure Chest*, *Caper's Choicest*, etc.

The magazine published fiction by such names as Harlan Ellison.

Captivate

Comet Publications, Los Angeles CA.

1960's. More than 1 issue exists?

Caress

Rilgac Publishing Co., Hollwyood CA.

Early 1960's. At least 3 issues.

Pictorials, nonfiction, fiction.

Carnival

October/November 1950 – February/March 1951. 3 issues.

Nonfiction, pictorials.

Carnival

'A magazine of excitement.'

Show Magazine Inc., Chicago IL.

Black and white interiors. Digest-sized.

1953 – 1956? 20+ issues?

Nonfiction, pictorials.

Carnival

Magtab Publishing, New York NY.

September 1962 – November 1968? 26 issues?

Pictorials, fiction, nonfiction.

There appear to have been at least 3 or 4 men's magazines titled *Carnival* during the relevant time period.

Candlelight

Caper

Caper

Caper

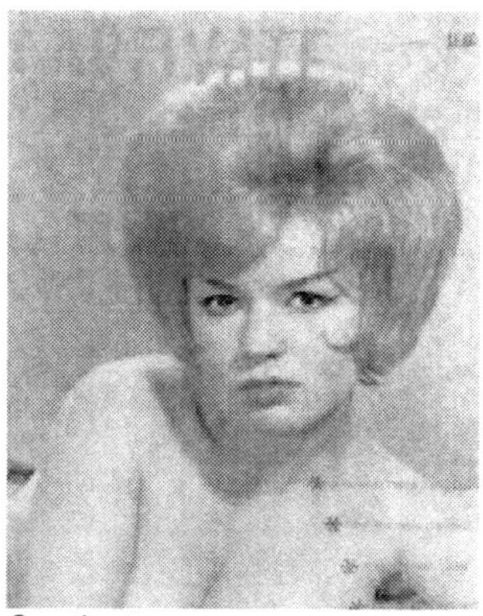
Captivate

Caress

Carnival (1950)

Carnival (1953)

Carnival (1962)

Carnival

1969. More than 2 issues published?

Pictorials, fiction, nonfiction, cartoons.

Was this a continuation of the previous Magtab title? Or perhaps an American edition of the British title from publishers City Magazines Ltd.?

Cartoon Comedy-Parade

Humorama Inc., New York NY (Atlas).

Black and white interiors. Measures 5.5 by 7.5 inches.

1963. 5 issues.

Cartoons, pictorials.

Cartoon Fun and Comedy

A retitling of *Cartoon Parade* – see next entry.

Cartoon Parade

Humorama Inc., New York NY (Atlas).

Black and white interiors. Measures 5.5 by 7.5 inches.

1960 – 1975. 77 issues.

Cartoons, pictorials.

This became *Cartoon Fun and Comedy* between Winter 1966 and Fall 1967, and all issues going forward with the July 1975 issue.

Casanova

Aries Publishing Co.

May 1957. Only 1 issue published?

Pictorials, nonfiction, fiction.

Casanova

Nova Publishing, New York NY.

January 1961. Only 1 issue published?

Pictorials, articles, cartoons.

Casbah

'The magazine for any man.'

Casbah Publishing Co., New York NY.

July 1959 – ? How many issues?

Pictorials.

Casbah

American Art Enterprises, Hollywood CA.

1961. How many issues produced?

Pictorials.

Carnival (1962)

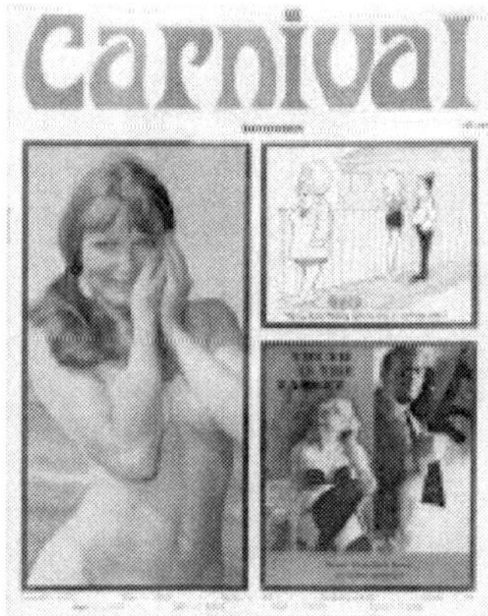

Carnival (1969)

Carnival (1969)

Cartoon Comedy Parade

Cartoon Comedy Parade

Cartoon Parade

Cartoon Parade

Casanova (1957)

Casanova (1961)

Cavalcade

Skye Publishing Co., New York NY.

March 1958 – 1979? 100+ issues.

Articles, pictorials.

The previous four issues (April 1957 – January 1958) were called *Man's Cavalcade*.

Cavalcade of Burlesque

Burlesque Historical Co., Philadelphia PA.

Black and white interiors.

1951 – 1954? 13 issues.

Pictorials.

Cavalier

Fawcett Publications, Greenwich CT; Arizill Realty and Publishing Co.

November 1952 – 1990's? 100+ issues, including Yearbooks.

Articles, pictorials.

Fawcett published this title until sometime in 1967, whereupon it was taken over by Arizill.

Celebrate

Ken Publishing Co., Studio City CA.

Black-and-white and color interior.

No date. One-shot?

Pictorials, fiction, nonfiction.

This curiosity contains no indicia, only a small paragraph on the top right of the inside front cover, 'This Magazine is Published By: / Ken Publishing Co. / 11144 Ventura Blvd. / Studio City, Calif.' Since no zip code is given, and judging by the photos and content, this was probably produced before 1963, probably about 1960-61.

Celebrity

Black and white interiors. Measures 4 by 6 inches.

May 1954 – February 1956. 21 issues.

Nonfiction, pictorials.

As the title suggests, this was a pocket-sized mag devoted to celebrity news and gossip, with some decent pictorials thrown in so as to include it here.

Challenge For Men

Almat / Pyramid.

March 1955 – October 1959. 30 issues.

Fiction and nonfiction.

Champ

Hillman Periodicals Inc., New York NY.

May 1957 – January 1958. 5 issues.

Fiction and nonfiction.

Cavalcade

Cavalcade

Cavalcade

Cavalcade of Burlesque

Cavalier

Cavalier

Celebrate

Challenge For Men

Champ

Champagne
American Art Agency Inc., Hollywood CA (Parliament).
1961 – 1972? 20+ issues, including at least 1 Annual.
Pictorials.

Champion For Men
Stanley Publications, New York NY.
April 1959 – February 1960. 9 issues.
Fiction and nonfiction.

Charger
Candar Publishing Company Inc., New York NY.
1968 – 1971. 11 issues?
Pictorials, fiction, nonfiction.

Charlie Julian's Las Vegas...
See *Las Vegas...*

Charm Photography
Popular Library Inc., New York NY.
Black and white interiors.
1955 – 1957. 6 issues.

Cheeky
Triumph News Co. Inc., Van Nuys CA.
1967 – 1969. 8 issues.
Pictorials.

Cheesecake: An American Phenomenon
Hillman Periodicals Inc., New York NY.
1953. One-shot?
Pictorials, nonfiction, cartoons.

Chere
International Publications Inc., Hollywood CA.
Black and white interiors with color centerfold.
1962 – 1963? At least 5 issues produced.
Pictorials.

Cherie
Sampson Publishing and Distribution Co., New York NY.
Black and white interior, with color centerfold.
Early 1960's. More than 1 issue produced?
Pictorials, nonfiction.

Champagne

Champagne

Champion For Men

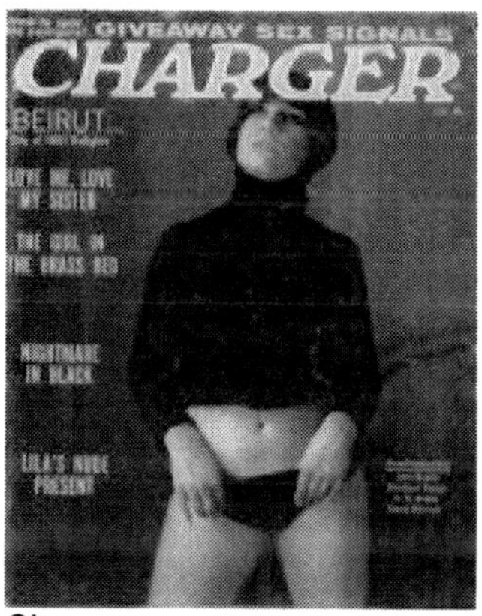

Charger

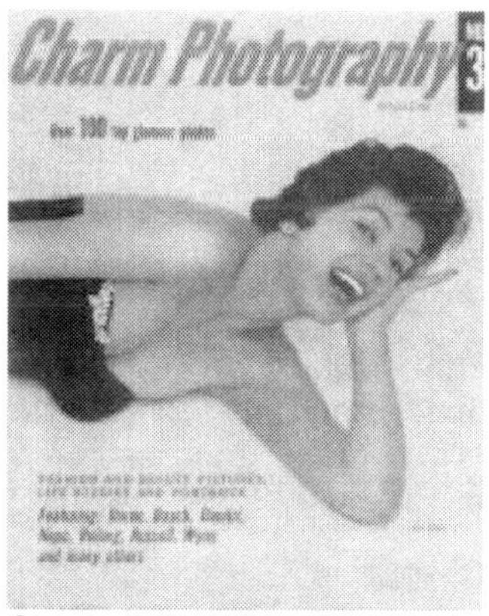

Charm Photography

Cheeky

Cheesecake

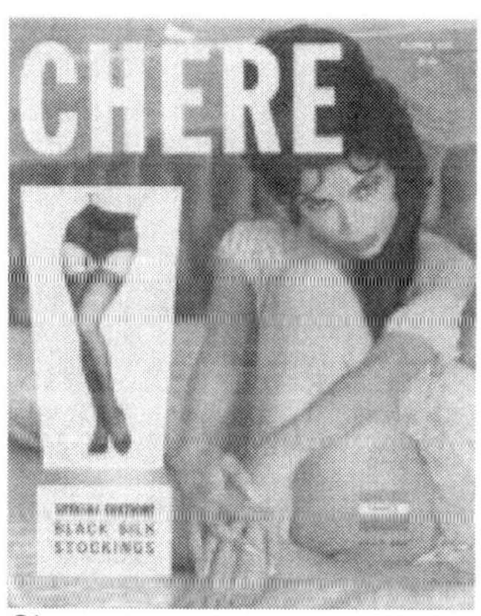

Chere

Cherie

Chez Paree
Bonanza Publishing Co., North Hollywood CA.
1962 – ? At least 1 issue published.
Pictorials, nonfiction.

Chic
Delilah Publishing Corp., New York NY.
Black and white interiors, with color centerfolds.
1962. More than 1 issue published?
Pictorials, nonfiction.

Chicks and Chuckles
Publication Management Corp., New York NY.
Black and white interiors.
June 1955 – 1963? 40+ issues.
Pictorials, cartoons.

CineFemmes
New Link Publications, Hollywood CA.
Black and white interiors.
1965 – 1967? At least 5 issues produced.
Pictorials, nonfiction, fiction.
Atlhough the title suggested that this magazine would focus upon female celebrities, it was mainly a pleasant mix of beautiful models and interesting articles with occasional fiction.

Clash
Unity Publishing.
July 1957. More than 1 issue?
Adventure fiction.

Classic Cat
Seven Seventy Publishers, North Hollywood CA.
Black and white interiors, with color photos.
1960's. How many issues published?
Pictorials, nonfiction.

Classic Photography
Arnold Magazines Inc., Stamford CT.
Black and white interiors.
1958 – 1958. 7 issues?
Pictorials, nonfiction.
Several issues feature photography by Russ Meyer, including a nice Diane Webber series in the Summer 1957 issue.

Chez Paree

Chicks and Chuckles

Chicks and Chuckles

CineFemmes

CineFemmes

ClassiC Cat

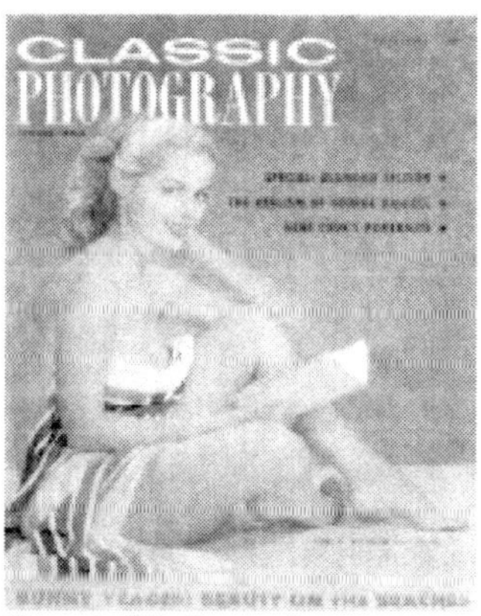

Classic Photography

Classic Photography

Classic Photography

Classy Nifty Nylons

See *Nifty Nylons*.

Classy Nylons

1960's. More than 1 issue published?

Click

American Art Agency Inc., Hollywood CA (Parliament).

1962 – 1964. 6 issues?

Pictorials.

Click

Antony Publications Inc., New York NY.

Black and white interiors, with color centerfolds.

1960's. How many issues produced?

Pictorials.

Climax

Macfadden Publications.

March – August 1953; April 1957 – October 1963? 80 issues?

Fiction and nonfiction.

The publishing history of this title is convoluted and confusing. There were initially five issues in 1953 before the magazine disappeared from the newsstands, reappearing in 1957. It would stay about 1964, at which time the title apparently changed to *Impact*. This would last until 1965 or '66, although an issue titled *Climax* and dated November 1966, v.14, #1, has been found... so, who can say.

Climax

Challenge Publications.

May 1968 – 1980. ~75 issues.

Pictorials.

Clingers

1960's. More than 1 issue?

Cloud 9

American Art Agency Inc., Hollywood CA (Parliament).

Black and white, and color photos.

1959 – 1972? ~30 issues?

Pictorials.

Clover

Comet Publications, Los Angeles CA.

1964 – 1967. At least 8 issues.

Pictorials, nonfiction, fiction.

Classy Nylons

Click (Parliament)

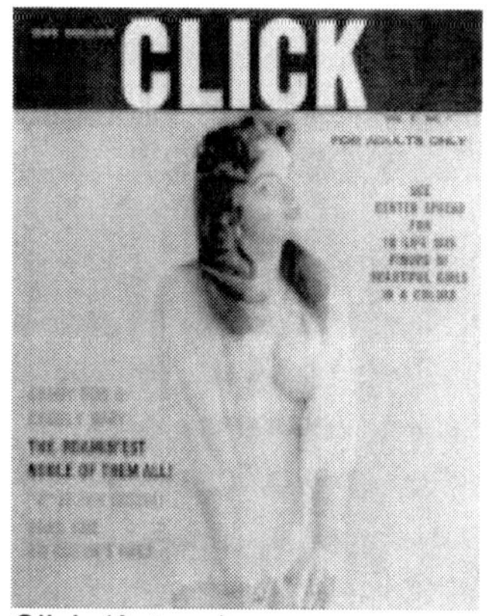

Click (Antony)

Climax (MacFadden)

Climax (MacFadden)

Climax (Challenge Pubs.)

Climax (Challenge Pubs.)

Cloud 9

Clover

Clyde

RGR Enterprises, New York NY.

September 1964 – ? Ran at least through 1967.

Nonfiction, pictorials, cartoons.

The February 1967 issue, probably the most easily found number, features Raquel Welch in a bikini on the cover.

Cocktail

Studio Publications, Inc., Studio City CA; American Art Agency, Hollywood CA.

1959 – early 1970's? At least 32 issues, plus at least one (1960) Calendar.

Pictorials, cartoons.

Note: The second issue (v.1, #2) was reprinted, with very little alteration, as *Cordial* #1 in 1962.

Color Pix

Color photos. Measures 5.5 by 8.5 inches.

Late 1950's? At least 3 issues.

Pictorials.

Combat

Banner Magazines, Inc.

Black and white interiors with occasional color. Measures 8.25 by 11 inches.

February – April 1959. 2 issues?

Adventure fiction.

Comedy

Humorama Inc., New York NY (Atlas).

Black and white interiors. Measures 5.5 by 7.5 inches.

1951 – 1964? 70+ issues?

Cartoons, pictorials.

Companion

Ladies' Coronet Inc., New York NY.

Black and white interiors. Measures 5.25 by 7 inches.

1960's. How many issues published?

Nonfiction, pictorials.

This was a Myron Fass magazine.

Complete Man

Atlas Magazines Inc., New York NY.

February 1965 – April 1967. 11 issues.

Adventure fiction.

Note: The former Atlas title *Ken For Men* had one issue from 1957 titled *Complete Man's Magazine*; and this one seems to have taken over the numbering of the former; but otherwise there doesn't seem to be much continuity between the two.

Clyde

Cocktail

Cocktail

Color Pix

Combat

Comedy

Comedy

Complete Man

Complete Man

Conflict
December 1955 – February 1956? 2 issues only?
Adventure fiction.

Connoisseur's World
Connoisseur Publications, Beverly Hills CA.
April 1964 – ?. At least 3 issues published?
Fiction, nonfiction, pictorials.

Conquest
See *Man's Conquest*.

Consent
American Art Agency Inc., Hollywood CA (Parliament).
1964 – 1965. 4 issues?
Pictorials.

Consent (2nd)
1960's. How many issues?

Consort
1960 – 1961. 2 issues published?

Contessa
1960's. More than 1 issue published?

Continental
Glo-Mar Publishing Co., New York NY (Sampson?).
Early 1960's. More than 1 issue published?
Pictorials, nonfiction.

Copper Cuties
January – August 1965? At least 5 issues published.
As the title would suggest, this magazine focused on darker-skinned ladies.
Did this title make a comeback in 1969?

Coquette
American Art Agency Inc., Hollywood CA (Parliament).
1963 – 1964. At least 4 issues published.
Pictorials.
There was another magazine by this title during the early 1970's by another publisher.

Conflict

Connoisseur's World

Consent (Parliament)

Consent (2nd)

Consort

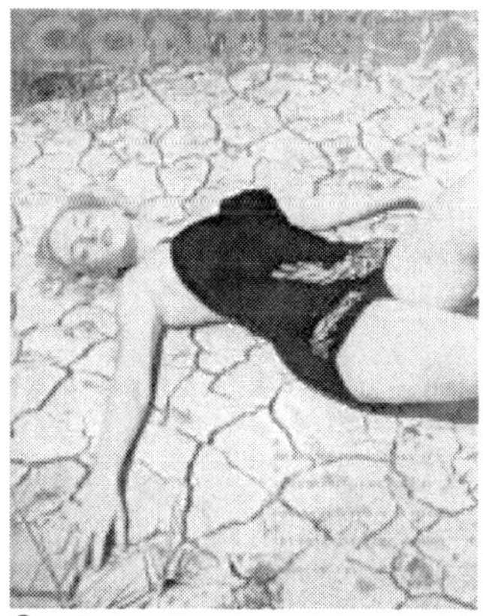
Contessa

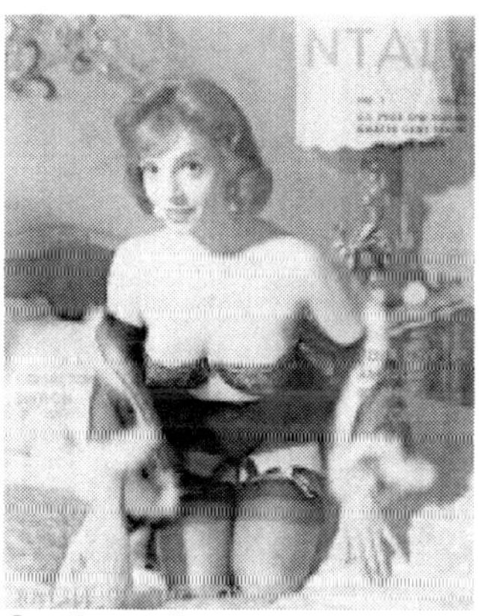
Continental

Copper Cuties

Coquette

Cordial
American Art Agency Inc., Hollywood CA (Parliament).
Black-and-white interior with color centerfold.
1962 – ? At least 2 issues.
Pictorials, drink recipes, cartoons.
The first issue is a virtual reprint of *Cocktail* v.1, #2.

Courage
Arnold Magazine Inc., New York NY.
November 1957 – April 1958. 3 issues.
Adventure fiction.

Cover Girls Models
Models Publishing Co. Inc., New York NY.
Black and white interiors.
November 1949 – August 1954. 26 issues.
Pictorials, nonfiction?

Cuddle
Seven Seventy Publishers, North Hollywood CA.
1960's. How many issues published?

Cuddle Bug
Early 1960's. At least 2 issues produced.

Cutie
American Art Agency Inc., Hollywood CA.
1962 – 1967? 5 issues?
Pictorials.

Dame
'There's nothing like a dame.'
Steele Publications.
Black and white interiors.
1961 – ? How many issues produced?
Nonfiction, pictorials, cartoons.

Dame Data
1960's. More than 1 issue produced?
This was a compilation magazine, made up of issues of other previous titles rebound together.

Cordial

Cordial

Courage

Courage

Cover Girls Models

Cover Girls Models

Cuddle Bug

Cuddle Bug

Dame Data

Dames

'There's nothing like 'em!'

Imperial Publishing Co., Hollywood CA.

Black and white interior with color centerfold.

1962. More than 1 issue produced?

Dandy

1963. More than 1 issue produced?

Dandy in Hose

Tri-S Publications, Hollywood CA.

1964. More than 1 issue produced?

Pictorials.

V.1 #2 acknowledged. Is this simply a continuation of 1963's *Dandy*?

Danger

June – September 1959? Only 2 issues?

Adventure fiction.

Dapper

Magnum-Royal Publications, New York NY; Sunway Periodicals, Chatsworth CA.

April 1965 – 1982? ~100 issues plus several giant-sized special issues.

Pictorials, nonfiction.

Dare

'The magazine that dares to tell the truth.'

YOU Publications, New York NY.

Black and white interiors. Measures 4 by 6 inches.

November 1952 – 1960? 35+ issues.

Nonfiction, pictorials.

Daring

Candar Publishing Co., New York NY.

February 1967 – 1975? 50 issues?

Pictorials.

Formerly the adventure-fiction publication *Man's Daring*, with the Feb. 1967 issue it debuted as a girlie magazine with photo covers.

Daring Dolls

Health Knowledge Inc., New York NY.

1968 – 1971. 8 issues published?

Pictorials.

Dames

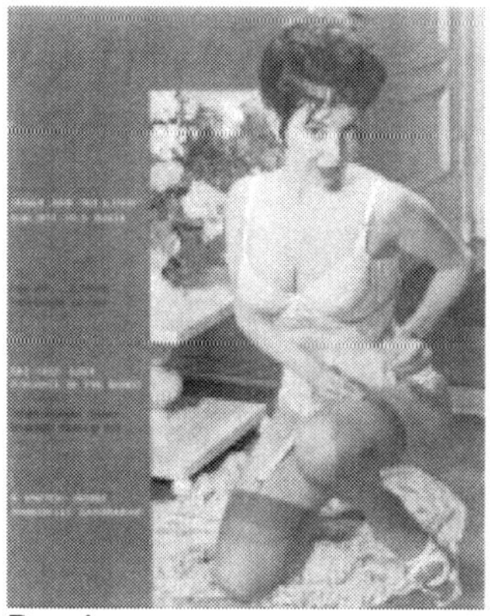
Dandy

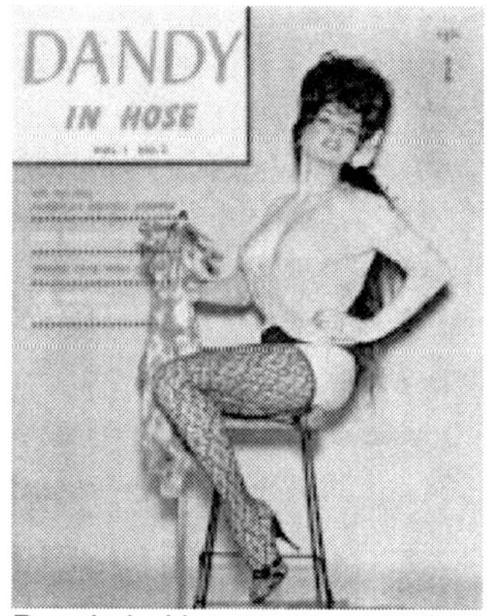

Dandy In Hose

Dapper

Dapper

Dare

Daring

Daring

Daring Dolls

Dar'lin

1960's. How many issues were published?

Dash

American Art Agency Inc., Hollywood CA (Parliament).

1960's? At least 5 issues published.

Pictorials.

Date Mates

Bruce-Royal Publishing, Derby CT.

1964 – 1965? How many issues published?

Dazzle

'Diversting damsels daringly delineated.'

Ken Publishing, Studio City CA; Dazzle Publications.

1957 – 1958? At least 5 issues.

Nonfiction, pictorials, cartoons.

Debonair

Stanley Publications, New York NY; Debonair Publications, New York NY.

December 1960 – February 1961; November 1964 – 1980? 100+ issues, including 3 specials.

Pictorials, fiction, nonfiction.

Apparently two issues were put out in 1960-61 before the title was relaunched in Nov. 1964 with v.1, #1, then again with a new v.1 #1 starting in December 1971.

Delight

1962 – 1964? How many issues were produced?

Delite

Caesar Publishers Inc., New York NY.

1962 – 1965. ~10 issues.

Pictorials.

Demoiselle

Sampson Publishing and Distribution Co., New York NY.

1962. More than 1 issue exists?

Pictorials.

Demure

1960's. How many issues were published?

Dash

Date Mates

Dazzle

Debonair

Debonair

Debonair

Delite

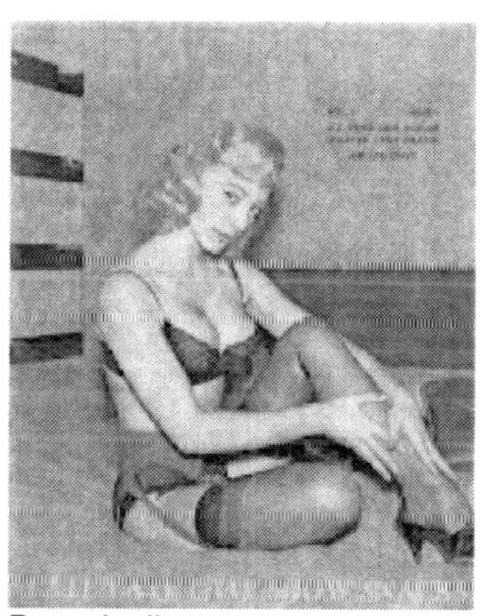

Demoiselle

Demure

Desire
Caesar Publishers Inc., New York NY; Patra Publications, New York NY.
1962 – 1965? How many issues were produced?
Pictorials.
Not to be confused with a gay men's magazine with the same title.

Devil
'One hell of a magazine.'
1960's. How many issues were produced?

Diabolique
Selbee Associates Inc., New York NY.
Black and white interiors, with color centerfolds.
1960's. At least 3 issues published.
Pictorials, nonfiction, fiction.

Diamond Stud
Comet Publications, Los Angeles CA.
Black and white interiors with color centerfolds.
Early 1960's. How many issues were produced?
Pictorials, fiction, nonfiction.
Mainly black-and-white nude photo shoots with some fiction in-between.
Note: Was there more than one magazine with this title during this time?

Dollies
Triumph News Co., North Hollywood CA.
1967 – 1969? At least 4 issues published.
Pictorials, nonfiction, fiction.

Dolls
1960's. How many issues were produced?

Dolls & Dolls
American Art Agency Inc., Hollywood CA (Parliament).
1960's – 1970's? At least 8 issues produced.
Pictorials.

Don Juan
Art Enterprises Inc., Los Angeles CA.
1959 – 1962? 5 issues publishes?

Don Juan
EmTee Publishing, New York NY.
1964 – ? How many issues were produced?

Desire

Devil

Diabolique

Diamond Stud

Dollies

Dolls

Dolls and Dolls

Don Juan (Art Ent.)

Don Juan (Emtee)

Dream

Orly Publications Ltd., New York NY.

1962 – 1963? At least 3 issues published?

Dude

Mystery Publishing Co., New York NY; Dugent Publishing Corp., New York NY.

August 1956 – 1981? 100+ issues (incl. at least 2 Annual/Specials).

Pictorials, nonfiction, fiction.

Earlier issues were more of a 'slick' men's magazine in the style of *Playboy* – upscale, respectable, a nice blend of features with semi-nude photography; sometime in the late 60's or early 70's it became almost an exclusively pictorial mag with sex-oriented articles.

Duel

Summer 1957. Only 1 issue published?

Adventure fiction.

Duke

Duke Publishing Co., Chicago IL.

June – November 1957. 6 issues?

Nonfiction, fiction, pictorials.

This is one of the great What Might Have Beens of the men's magazine world. It was basically a *Playboy* for black men, with a strong emphasis on African-American interests, but from a decidedly upscale point-of-view. Issues contained a healthy mix of fiction and nonfiction (the first issue contained work by Erskine Caldwell and Langston Hughes) with a few girlie photo spreads, as well as humor (including a Ray Bradbury story) and even poetry. Unfortunately, it must not have sold very well, because it didn't last longer than six months.

Note: A second magazine called *Duke* was released starting in 1967; it has no relation to this one.

Duke

M.F. Enterprises, New York NY.

Color interiors.

April 1967 – 1978? ~80 issues, plus at least 3 giant-sized special issues.

Pictorials, nonfiction.

Duo

World Wide News Co., Cleveland OH.

1960's. More than 1 issue published?

Pictorials.

Dusty

Delilah Publishing Corp., New York NY.

Early 1960's. How many isses were published?

Dream

Dream

Dude

Dude

Dude

Duke (1957)

Duke (1967)

Duke (1967)

Duo

Earl Wilson's Album of Showgirls

Skye Publishing Co., New York NY.

Black and white with color centerfold. Measures 8.25 by 10.75 inches.

1956. One-shot?

Pictorials.

This was a magazine devoted to photos of various celebrated models and strippers of the day, with humorous commentary (and purported interviews) by noted columnist Earl Wilson.

Ecstasy

1960's. How many issues produced?

Pictorials.

Eden

'For the urbane male.'

Jaro Publishers, New York NY.

Late 1950's? More than 1 issue published?

Not to be confused with the nudist publication.

Elmer's Naked Jungle

Press Arts Inc., Canoga Park CA.

1969. At least 2 issues published.

This was a hose-and-garters fetish magazine. The title referred to photographer Elmer Batters, who was known for this predilection.

Epic

Skye Publishing Co., New York NY.

March 1957 – June 1959; February – June 1961. 12 issues.

Adventure fiction and nonfiction.

Apparently the magazine was restarted for 3 issues in 1961 after having been cancelled two years previous.

Erotica 1

International Publications Inc., Hollywood CA.

Black and white interiors.

1963 – ? How many issues published?

Pictorials, fiction, nonfiction.

This was a very cheaply produced publication that made use of public-domain material in order to fill out the pages without spending too much money.

Escapade

Dee Publishing Co., Los Angeles CA; Bruce-Royal Publishing, Derby CT.

October 1955 – 1983? 100+ issues, plus several large-size special issues.

Nonfiction, fiction, pictorials.

Special issues fell under such titles as *Escapade's Best*, *Escapade's Choicest*, and *Escapade's Carnival* in addition to the usual Annual and Yearbook ones.

Earl Wilson's...

Ecstasy

Ecstasy

Epic

Epic

Escapade

Escapade

Escapade

Escapade

Escape To Adventure

Escape Magazines, Inc.

July 1957 – November 1964. 41 issues.

Adventure fiction.

Europe's Top Pin-Ups

Library Enterprises.

1954 – 1957. 4 issues.

Eve

'The woman's magazine for men.'

1950 – 1951. 6 issues.

Nonfiction, pictorials?

Eve

Sampson Publishing and Distribution Co., New York NY.

Black and white with color centerfold.

1962 – ? At least 8 issues produced.

Note: There are two issues of this title numbered v.1 #1. The (apparently) earlier one has a squarish orange title logo, while the later one features the leaf-logo symbol seen on all other covers in this series.

Exclusive

Digest Publications Inc., New York NY.

Black and white interiors. Measures 6 by 9 inches.

1950's. 10+ issues?

Nonfiction, pictorials.

Exotic Adventures

Gladiator Publications.

1958 – 1959. 6 issues.

Adventure fiction.

Exotica

Selbee Associates Inc., New York NY.

Black and white interiors, with color centerfolds.

1960's? At least 2 issues produced.

Pictorials, nonfiction, fiction.

Expose

Skye Publishing Co., New York NY.

June 1959 – December 1960. 9 issues under this title.

Adventure fiction.

This title was called *Sensation* for three issues previously.

Escape to Adventure

Escape to Adventure

Europe's Top Pin-Ups

Eve (1950)

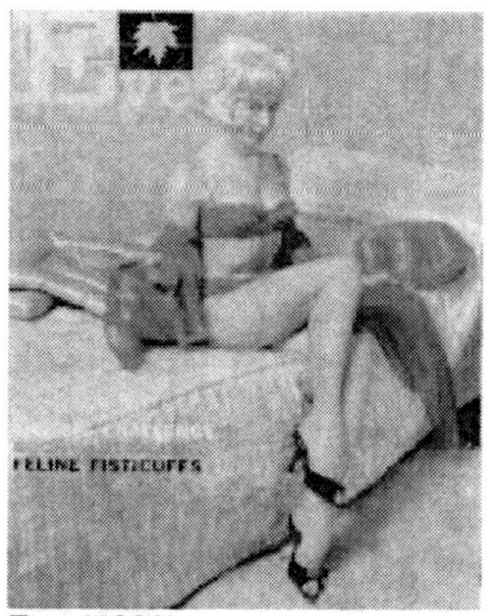

Eve (1962)

Exclusive

Exotic Adventure

Exotica

Expose

Eye

Mutual Magazine Corp., New York NY (Atlas).

May 1949 – June 1956; February – December 1960. ~60 issues.

Pictorials, nonfiction, cartoons.

This Atlas title was a general-interest men's digest with features, sports, and non-nude girlie photos through its run in the 1950's; it was briefly reintroduced in 1960 featuring cartoons and girlie photos.

Eye (2nd)

1966 – 1969? ~15 issues.

Nonfiction, pictorials.

Eyeful

Eyeful Magazine Inc., New York NY.

March 1943 – 1955. ~65 issues.

Pictorials.

Early good-girl photo and art mag.

Eyeful

1964. More than 2 issues published?

Pictorials, nonfiction, fiction.

Eyeful of Fun

Humorama Inc., New York NY (Atlas).

1960's? How many issues?

Black and white interiors. Measures 5.5 by 7.5 inches.

Fabulous Females

There seems to have been several different magazines from different publishers produced under this title throughout the 1950's. These were invariably pinup mags featuring black-and-white nonnude and semi-nude photos. The most common issue seems to be the #1 from 1955. Publishers for these include Riviera Pin-Up Corp., Literary Enterprises Inc., and Sampson Publishing Co.

Note that there was a separate magazine under this title from the 1970's, with more pornographic nude photo sets.

Fabulous Femmes

N.M. Publications Inc., New York NY.

1962 – 1963. At least 6 issues produced.

Pictorials.

Fair Sex, The

'The magazine for girl watchers.'

Frimac Publications, North Hollywood CA.

1962. More than 1 issue published?

Pictorials.

Eye (Atlas)

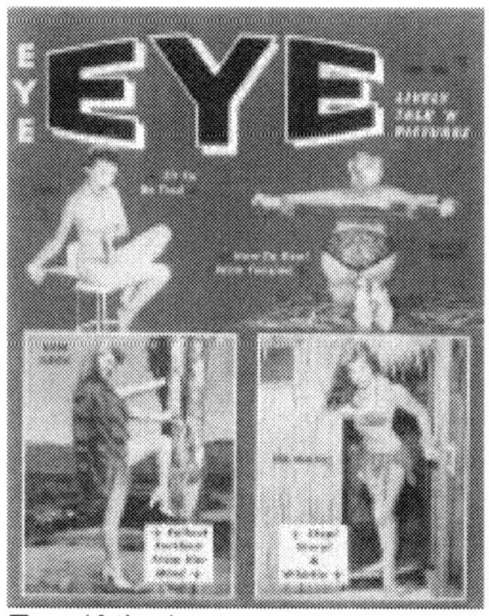

Eye (Atlas)

Eye (2nd)

Eyeful (1943)

Eyeful (1964)

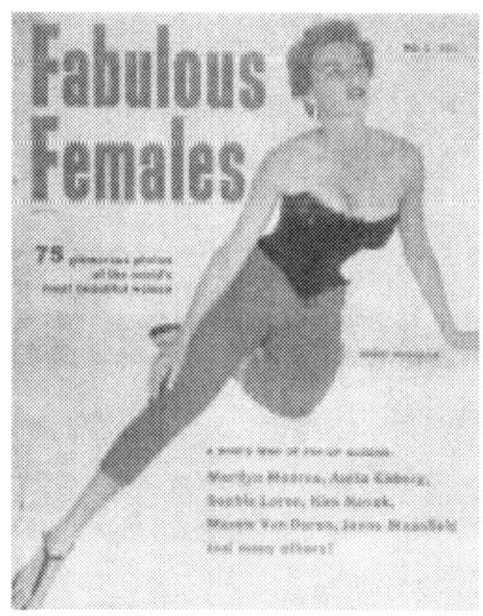

Fabulous Females

Fabulous Femmes

Fabulous Femmes

The Fair Sex

Fame
Dodshaw Publishing Corp., New York NY.
Pocket-sized.
1955. 5 issues.
Nonfiction, pictorials.

Famous Models
Volitant Publishing Corp., New York NY.
1950 – 1951. 9 issues.
Nonfiction, pictorials.

Famous Paris Models
Volitant Publishing Corp., New York NY.
December 1951 – February 1953. 8 issues.
Pictorials, nonfiction.

Fantasy & Lace
Comet Publications, Los Angeles CA.
1960's. How many issues were published?

Feline
1960's. How many issues were published?

Female Fiesta
American Art Agency Inc., Hollywood CA (Parliament).
1966 – 1968? At least 6 issues published.
Pictorials.

Female Temptress
1960's. More than 1 issue?
Pictorials, nonfiction.
This was a compilation title, made up of rebound copies of other magazines.

Femina
American Art Agency Inc., Hollywood CA (Parliament).
1969 – ? Several issues published.
Pictorials.

Feminine Form
Monogram Publications, Los Angeles CA.
October 1958 – 1959. ~10 issues.
Pictorials.

Famous Paris Models

Fantasy and Lace

Feline

Female Fiesta

Female Fiesta

Female Temptress

Femina

Feminine Forme

Feminine Form

Festival

Early 1960's. How many issues published?

Fever

Zee Zee Publishing, New York NY.

1959. At least 2 issues published.

Pictorials, nonfiction.

This was actually a teaser booklet (a 'pitchbook') handed out at burlesque houses to promote certain performers and acts. 'Zee Zee Publishing' was actually the work of Zee Zee Martine, herself a burlesque performer.

Figure

Amateur Art and Camera, Chicago IL.

1954 – 1959. ~25 issues.

Did this combine with *Amateur Screen and Photography* to become the next entry?

Figure Art

Camerarts Publishing Co., Chicago IL.

1959 – 1960. 6 issues.

Pictorials.

This was a retitling of the previous *Amateur Screen and Photography.*

Figure File

Camerarts Publishing Co., Chicago IL.

Black and white interiors. Measures 5.5 by 8.5 inches.

1958. 6 regular issues plus 1 Annual?

Pictorials.

(Danny Rouzer's) Figure Photography

Walter D. Rouzer Jr., Hollywood CA.

1958. One-shot.

This one-off was published by one of the minor glamour photographers of the era. The 'Walter D. Rouzer Jr.' listed as publisher is the same person as the 'Danny Rouzer' in the title.

Figure Photography (and Darkroom Guide)

July 1957 – ? How many issues published?

Figure Photography Annual/Quarterly

Publisher's Development

1950's – 1970's. 86 issues.

Pictorials.

This magazine went through several small title changes during its lifetime, but kept the basic configuration.

Note that although each issue was numbered sequentially, not all of them featured the number on the cover.

Festival

Fever

Figure

Figure Art

Figure Photography (1st)

Figure Photography (2nd)

Figure Photography (2nd)

Figure Photography (2nd)

Figure Photography (2nd)

Figure Studies Annual
Camerarts Publishing Co., Chicago IL.
1949 – 1966. ~16 issues.
Pictorials.

Figurette
Camerarts Publishing Co., Chicago IL.
Winter 1958 – Winter 1961. 13 issues.
Pictorials.

Film & Figure
Jaybird Enterprises, Hollywood CA (Parliament).
1965 – 1978? ~50 issues.
Pictorials.

Flame
'Fiery females.'
Art Enterprises Inc., Los Angeles CA.
Black and white interiors.
1959 – 1961. ~ 10 issues.
Nonfiction, pictorials, cartoons.

Flash News Illustrated
Correspondent News Service, Sparta IL.
1964. More than 2 issues produced?
Nonfiction, pictorials.
Though not sporting a cover price, this was apparently a scandal mag that existed for however brief a time. The stories were incredibly sensationalistic ("Jungle Boy Brought Up By Apes," "Witches Are Prowling Europe Today") but there were also a number of cheesecake girlie photos.

Flaunt
1960's. More than 6 issues published?
Pictorials.

Fling (Festival)
Relim Publishing Co., Chicago IL.
1957 – 1996. 100+ issues, plus various giant-sized special issues.
Pictorials, nonfiction.
Billed as men's 'passport to pleasure,' this magazine stayed true to its girlie-mag origins even when it went through a more general *Playboy*-like phase during the mid-60's.
Note: It was titled *Fling Festival* for part of its run.

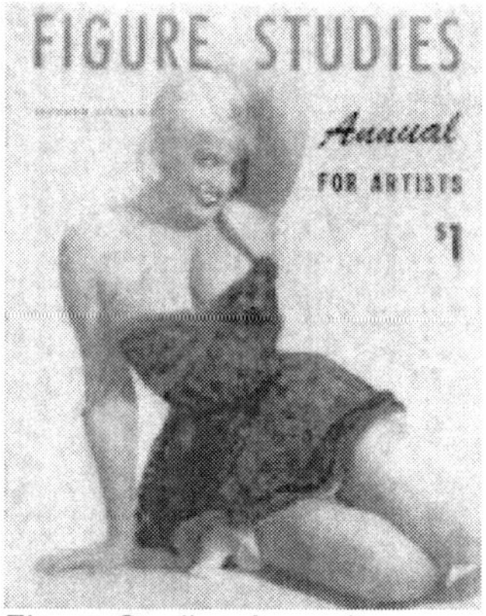

Figure Studies Annual

Figure Studies Annual

Film and Figure

Flame

Flash News Illustrated

Flaunt

Fling

Fling

Fling

Flip

'And make them come to life.'

Hillman Periodicals Inc., New York NY.

Black and white interiors.

1955. One-shot.

Pictorials, nonfiction.

This was an ingenious concept for a girlie/glamour photo magazine. The edges of each interior page featured small film stills of various beautiful women engaged in different activities, printed in sequence, so that the reader could riffle through the pages and the resulting images could be seen as 'moving,' much like the frames in a film.

Flip

Flip Publishing Co., North Hollywood CA.

1961 – ? How many issues?

Pictorials, nonfiction.

Not to be confused with the later teen-idol mag.

Flirt

Flirt Magazine Inc., New York NY.

December 1947 – April 1955. 44 issues.

Pictorials, nonfiction, cartoons.

This magazine, which started in the 1940's, kept its focus on good-girlie photo sessions with a sense of humor, throughout its entire run.

Flirt

Franklin Publications, North Hollywood CA.

1962 – 1963? 3 issues?

Pictorials, nonfiction.

Flirt 'n Skirt

This appears to have been a British magazine from the late 60's - mid 70's; but some issues have a dollar-denominated price on the cover, probably to sell here in the States.

Focus

Atlas Magazines Inc., New York NY.

December 1949 – 1957? ~80 issues.

Pictorials, nonfiction.

Marilyn Monroe appeared on the cover of the May 1953 issue.

Focus On...

Selbee Associates Inc., New York NY; Health Knowledge Inc., New York NY.

1963 – ? 5+ issues?

Pictorials.

This magazine was about a different related subject with each issue. For example, #1 was 'Focus on Bettie Page,' #2 was 'Focus on London After Dark,' #3 was 'Focus on Strip Tease Around the World,' etc.

Flip (1961)

Flip (1961)

Flirt (1st)

Flirt (1st)

Flirt (2nd)

Flirt and Skirt

Focus

Focus

Focus On...

Follies

'A gay all girl revue.'

1950 – 1951. 2 issues?

Pictorials.

Follies

Gildpoint Ltd.; Magtab Publishing Corp., New York NY.

Black and white interior with color centerfold.

November 1956 – 1972? ~75 issues?

This long-running magazine featured pretty much nothing but scantily clad beautiful women, with the last few years of the title going into the realm of full nudity.

For Men Only

Atlas Magazines Inc. (under various publisher names), New York NY.

May 1954 – 1980? 100+ issues, including several Annuals.

Primarily fiction.

One of the top men's fiction magazines during its heyday.

Foto

Arena Publishing Corp., New York NY.

April 1950 – January 1951. 5 issues.

Pictorials, nonfiction.

Foto Parade

Foto Parade Inc., New York NY.

Black and white interiors. Measures 10 by 13 inches.

December 1949 – 1951. At least 6 issues published.

Pictorials, nonfiction.

A young Marilyn Monroe appeared on the cover of the first issue.

Foto-Rama

Arena Publishing Corp., New York NY.

Black and white interiors. Digest-sized.

January 1953 – 1973? 100+ issues.

Pictorials, nonfiction.

French Follies

American Art Agency Inc., Hollywood CA (Parliament).

1963 – 1970. 25 issues?

French Frills

American Art Agency Inc., Hollywood CA (Parliament).

1960 – 1969. 31 issues plus 1 giant-sized Jumbo Edition.

Pictorials.

Follies (1950)

Follies (1956)

For Men Only

For Men Only

Foto

Foto Parade

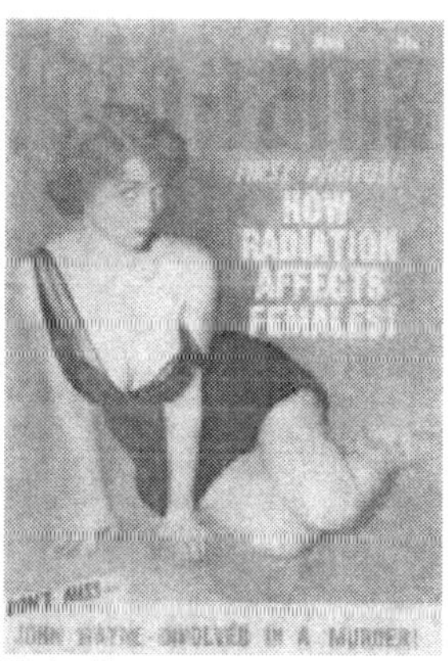

Foto-Rama

French Follies

French Frills

French Frolic

Sampson Publishing and Distribution Co., New York NY.

Black and white interior, with color centerfold.

Early 1960's. More than 1 issue produced?

Pictorials.

French Fun

Health Knowledge Inc., New York NY.

1967 – 1970. 5 issues?

Pictorials.

French Lace

'The continental boudoir.'

Black and white, and color interiors.

1960's. How many issues produced?

There are at least 2 issues of this title, neither of which has a volume or number or date listed on the cover, although both have the motto 'The Continental Boudoir' so they are undoubtedly part of the same series.

French Pastry

Sampson Publishing and Distribution Co., New York NY.

Early 1960's. More than 1 issue produced?

Pictorials.

Note that there was a later, much more pornographic magazine with this same title.

French Sauce

Sampson Publishing and Distribution Co., New York NY.

Early 1960's. More than 1 issue published?

Pictorials.

French Spice

Sampson Publishing and Distribution Co., New York NY.

1962 – 1964? ~8 issues.

Pictorials.

Frenchy

Sari Publishing Co., North Hollywood CA.

Black and white interiors.

1962 – ? At least 5 issues.

Pictorials, nonfiction, cartoons.

Frenchy

Seven Seventy Publishers, North Hollywood CA.

1960's. At least 5 issues.

French Frolic

French Lace

French Pastry

French Sauce

French Spice

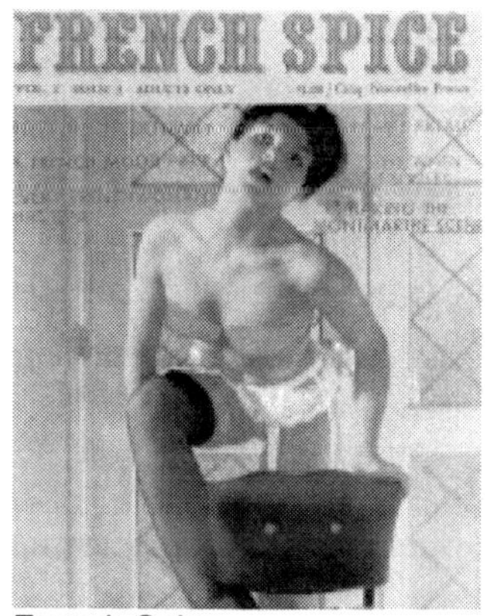

French Spice

Frenchy (Sari)

Frenchy (Sari)

Frenchy (770)

Frolic

Carnival Magazine Corp., New York NY.

May 1951 – 1973? 100+ issues.

Pictorials.

From beginning to end, this magazine basically only dealt with semi-nude pictorials and other sexually themed material.

Fun House

'A laugh picnic.'

Humorama Inc., New York NY (Atlas).

Black and white interiors. Measures 5.5 by 7.5 inches.

1964 – 1981? 50+ issues.

Cartoons, pictorials.

Funtasia

Actual Publishing Co., New York NY.

1957. 1 issue.

Humor, cartoons, pictorials.

Fury

Weider Publications, Jersey City NJ.

August 1953? – January 1964? 50+ issues.

Fiction originally, later fiction, nonfiction, and pictorials.

The publishing history of this magazine is unclear. The earliest confirmed issue seems to be August 1953, but with 'v.19, #5' indicated within. What magazine did this continue from?

Note: In 1962 this title's covers changed – as did nearly all men's magazines' – from painted adventure scenes to photographs, this time of young women.

Gaiete

Sampson Publishing and Distribution Co., New York NY.

Black and white interior with color centerfold.

1962. At least 2 issues.

Pictorials.

Gala

'America's greatest array of glamor.'

Gala Magazine Corp., New York NY.

1950? – 1973? 100+ issues.

Pictorials.

Gallant

Kapps Publications Inc., New York NY.

May 1959. Only 1 issue published?

Pictorials, nonfiction, cartoons.

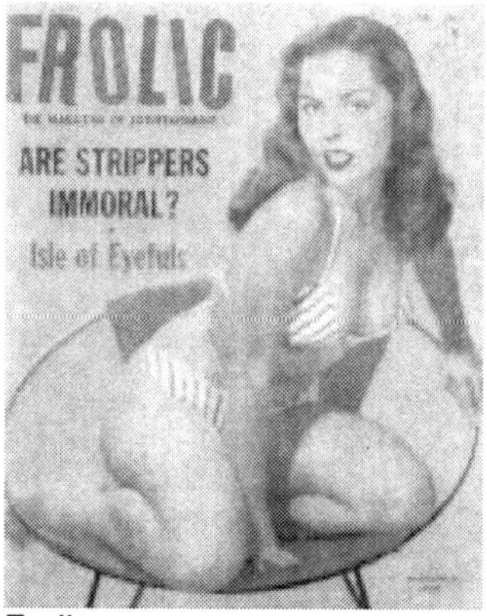

Frolic

Frolic

Fun House

Funtasia

Fury

Fury

Gaiete

Gala

Gallant

Gals A Go Go

American Art Agency Inc., Hollywood CA (Parliament).

1960's. More than 1 issue published?

Pictorials.

Gals and Gags

Health Knowledge Inc., New York NY.

1967 – 1971? ~20 issues.

Cartoons, pictorials.

Gals Galore

American Art Agency Inc., Hollywood CA (Parliament).

Late 1960's? ~10 issues.

Pictorials.

Gambling Vixens

Selbee Associates Inc., New York NY.

Black and white interiors. Measures 5.25 by 8.25 inches.

1964. More than 1 issue published?

Pictorials.

This curious little title doesn't technically fit into this volume, due to its not carrying a price on the cover (the method of distribution being unknown to this author), but since it's by Selbee Associates, and given the interesting combination of subjects, it is being included.

What does the 'C-23' on the cover signify? Was there a series of small booklets from Selbee like this?

Gay Blade

Bachelor Magazines Inc., New York NY.

Black and white interior with color centerfold.

December 1956 – May 1959? 4 issues?

Fiction, nonfiction, pictorials, cartoons.

Gay Book

1950's. More than 2 issues published?

Gayety

Phoenix Publications, Los Angeles CA.

1961. 2 issues?

Pictorials, nonfiction.

Gaze

Humorama Inc., New York NY (Atlas).

Black and white interiors. Measures 5.5 by 7.5 inches.

1955 – 1970's. ~100 issues.

Pictorials, cartoons.

Gals A GoGo

Gals Galore

Gals Galore

Gambling Vixens

Gay Blade

Gay Blade

Gayety

Gaze

Gaze

Gee-Whiz!

Humorama Inc., New York NY (Atlas).

Black and white interiors. Measures 5.5 by 7.5 inches.

September 1955 – late 1960's? 50+ issues.

Pictorials, cartoons.

Gem

Body Beautiful Publications Inc., Jersey City NJ.

January 1968 – 1990's? 100+ issues.

Pictorials, nonfiction.

Gent

Excellent Publications, New York, NY; PAR Publications Inc., New York NY.

Black and white interior with some color pictorials.

September 1956 – 2000's. ? – 100+ issues, including some larger-size special issues.

Pictorials, fiction, nonfiction.

Through the 70's, it was a more mainstream men's magazine, although it dropped fiction at a certain point, and (like every other men's mag) eventually became purely pornographic.

Gentleman

Bruce-Royal Publishing, Derby CT.

1960's. ? – 25+ issues.

Pictorials, nonfiction.

Although not generally considered among the top vintage men's mags these days, *Gentleman* did feature some truly beautiful women issue after issue.

Girl Show

Health Knowledge Inc., New York NY.

Black and white interiors with color centerfold.

Late 1960's – early 70's? 7 issues?

Pictorials.

Girl Watcher

'A guide to girl watching.'

Bonanza Publishing Co., Canton OH.

Black and white interiors with occasional color.

March – June 1959. Only 2 issues apparently.

Pictorials, humor.

Although this title did indeed have (clothed) pictorials of various models and actresses, it was intended as a humor magazine. It was probably meant as a parody of the attitude shown in other men's mags of the time.

Girls

1960's. At least 6 issues.

Pictorials.

Gee-Whiz!

Gem

Gent

Gent

Gentleman

Gentleman

Girl Show

Girl Watcher

Girls

Girls A Go Go
Seven Seventy Publishers, North Hollywood CA.
1960's. How many issues published?

Girls At Play
Art Enterprises Inc., Los Angeles CA.
1957 – 1958? More than 2 issues published?

Girls Girls Girls (1st)
Early 1960's. More than 2 issues published?
Pictorials, nonfiction.

Girls Girls Girls
Health Knowledge Inc., New York NY.
Late 1960's. At least 3 issues.

Girls in Orbit
See *Orbit*.

Girls in the Boudoir
Art Enterprises Inc., Los Angeles CA.
1950's. More than 1 issue?
Pictorials.

Girls Model Directory
Late 1950's? At least 3 issues published.

Girls of the World
1968 – 1974. 60+ issues.

Girly Guide
American Art Agency Inc., Hollywood CA (Parliament).
Late 1960's? At least 2 issues published.
Pictorials.

Glamor Girl Photography
Black and white interiors.
1959. Apparently only 2 issues published.
Pictorials.

Glamor Parade
Actual Publishing Co., New York NY.
August 1956 – 1959. ~12 issues.
Pictorials.

Girls A Go-Go

Girls Girls Girls (1st)

Girls in the Boudoir

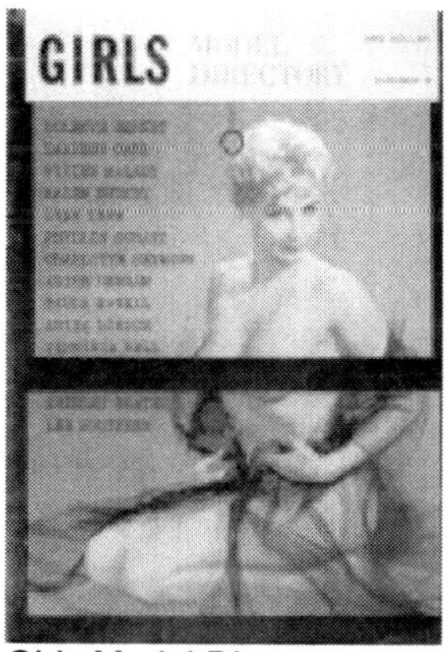

Girls Model Directory

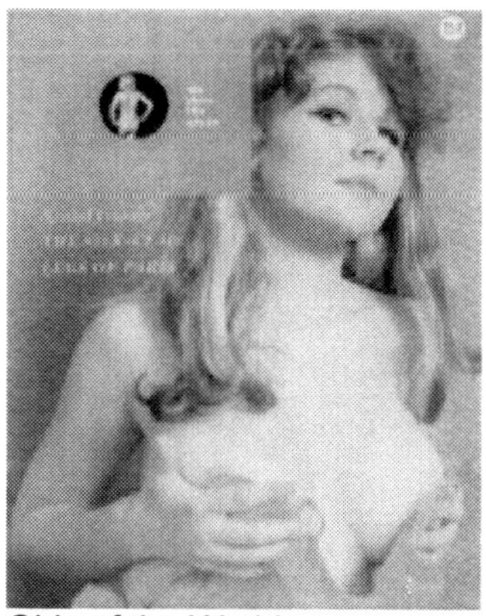
Girls of the World

Girly Guide

Glamor Girl Photography

Glamor Parade

Glamor Parade

Glamor Photography (1st)
1954 – 1957? ~5 issues?
Pictorials.

Glamor Photography
Magnum-Royal Publications, New York NY.
1967 – 1973. ~20 issues.
Pictorials, nonfiction.

Glamorous Girls
Bruce-Royal Publishing, Derby CT.
Winter 1963. Only 1 issue published?
Pictorials.

Glamorous Models
'The world's most alluring girls.'
Black and white interiors.
Mid-1940's – early 50's. ~40 issues?
Nonfiction, pictorials.

Glamour Photography
Glamour Photography, New York NY.
Black and white interiors.
1954 – 1957? At least 5 issues.
Pictorials, nonfiction.
This was apparently a semi-annual publication.

Glance
Headline Publications, New York NY.
1948 – 1953? ~35 issues.
Nonfiction, pictorials.

Glance
Cape Magazine Management Corp., New York NY.
1955? – 1960. ~30 issues?
Pictorials, nonfiction.
Is this a completely separate magazine from the one in the late 40's – early 50's?

Glo
Sampson Publishing and Distribution Co., New York NY.
1962. Only 1 issue published?

Glamor Photography (2nd)

Glamorous Girls

Glamorous Models

Glamorous Models

Glamour Photography

Glamour Photography

Glance (Headline)

Glance (Cape)

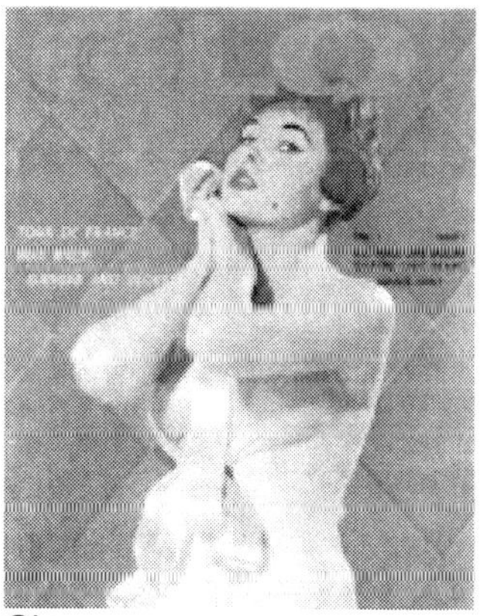

Glo

Go

A and B Associates, Los Angeles CA.

1965. More than 1 issue published?

Pictorials, nonfiction, fiction.

Go Big

Seven Seventy Publishers, North Hollywood CA.

1960's. At least 2 issues published.

Goddess

Black and white interior, with color centerfold.

1962. More than 1 issue published?

Pictorials.

Goddess

Skye Publishing Co., Inc., New York NY.

March 1968 – ? How many issues were published?

Pictorials, nonfiction, cartoons.

Godiva

1960's. How many issues published?

Good Humor

Capitol Stories Inc., Derby CT (Charlton).

1948 - 1980's. 100+ issues produced.

Pictorials, fiction, nonfiction, cartoons.

Possibly owing to Charlton's use of cheap materials, there should be more issues of this magazine surviving than there seem to be. Most of them are probably being sold in the Humor section rather than with the other men's mags, although the interiors consisted of both humor and pinups.

Good Times

'A revue of the world of pleasure.'

Barth Publishing Co., New York NY.

Black and white interiors. Measures 5 by 7.5 inches.

1953 – 1956. 20+ issues.

Pictorials, nonfiction, fiction.

Gorgeous Gals

American Art Agency Inc., Hollywood CA (Parliament).

Late 1960's? At least 4 issues published.

Groovy Girls

Dominion Publishing Co., North Hollywood CA.

Late 1960's. At least 10 issues published.

Go

Go Big

Go Big

Goddess

Godiva

Good Humor

Good Humor

Good Times

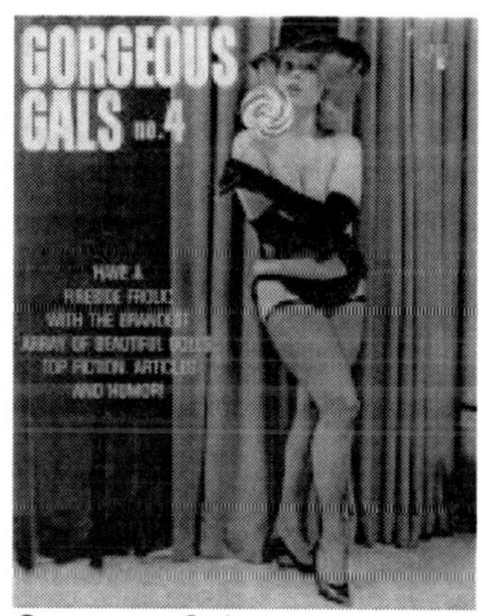

Gorgeous Gals

Gusto

'He-man adventures.'

Arnold Magazines Inc., Stamford CT.

October 1957 – February 1958. 3 issues.

Fiction, cartoons.

Gusto!

1962 – 1963? At least 4 issues.

Nonfiction, pictorials.

Guy

Banner Magazines Inc.

January – September, 1959. 5 issues.

Adventure fiction.

This title is apparently unrelated to the more successful one that came out four years later.

Guy

Pyramid Publications / Hewfred Publications.

October 1963 – July 1971. 44 isues, plus 3 Annuals.

Fiction, nonfiction, pictorials.

The 'multi-paneled' design of this magazine's covers makes it easy to spot.

Gypsy

Sampson Publishing and Distribution Co., New York NY.

Early 1960's. More than 1 issue published?

Not to be confused with a later, more pornographic mag.

Harem

1956 – 1960? Several issues published.

Apparently there were at least 3, maybe 4 different magazines (by different publishers?) published under this title from the 1950's to the 1980's. One of these, with the subtitle 'The magazine for sheiks,' sports the message 'Formerly *Lark* magazine' on the cover. Another, dated February 1957, features Jayne Mansfield on the cover.

Harem Holiday

American Art Agency Inc., Hollywood CA (Parliament).

1960's. At least 6 issues.

Pictorials.

This was apparently a repackaging, literally, of three or more other Parliament titles under one cover – that is, unsold copies of previous magazines were rebound together under the *Harem Holiday* cover, making this title's issues extra-thick and with a higher price tag.

Gusto (1st)

Gusto! (2nd)

Guy (Banner)

Guy (Pyramid)

Guy (Pyramid)

Gypsy

Harem

Harem

Harem Holiday

Harlequin / HQ

Magnum-Royal Publications, New York NY.

April 1963 – February 1965. 9 issues, plus 1 giant sized Special issue.

Fiction, nonfiction, pictorials.

This title was actually *Harlequin* on the cover for only 3 issues, then *HQ* for 5 more before becoming the long-running *Dapper* starting with the April 1965 issue.

He

'The magazine for men.'

HE Publications Inc., New York NY.

Measured 4 by 5.75 inches.

April 1953 – 1959? 35+ issues.

Nonfiction, pictorials.

Heatwave

1963. More than 1 issue published?

Heels & Hose

American Art Agency Inc., Hollywood CA (Parliament).

1962 – 1969? 25+ issues published.

Pictorials.

Hefty

Sari Publishing Co., North Hollywood CA; Press Arts Inc., Canoga Park CA.

1962 – 1968. ~20 issues.

Pictorials.

As the title suggests, this title was geared more toward models who had a little more meat on their bones, or who had somewhat larger breasts.

Hi-Life

Wilmot Enterprises, New York NY.

March 1958 – July 1965. ~40 issues plus at least 1 Special Edition.

Fiction, nonfiction, pictorials, cartoons.

Hi-Lite

Comet Publications, Los Angeles CA.

Early 1960's. How many issues produced?

Hi-Lite

Orly Publishing Co., New York NY.

Black and white interior, with color centerfold.

1962. One-shot?

Nonfiction, pictorials, fiction.

Harlequin

Harlequin / HQ

He

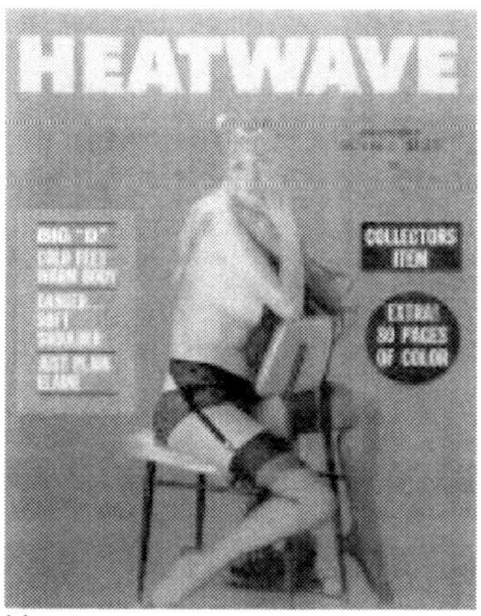

Heatwave

Heels and Hose

Hefty

Hi-Life

Hi-Lite (Comet)

Hi-Lite (Orly)

Hi-Lites

1960's. At least 10 issues?

Hi-Living

1960's. At least 5 issues.

Hi-Lo

Sampson Publishing and Distribution Co., New York NY.

Early 1960's? More than 1 issue published?

Hide & Seek

1965. More than 1 issue published?

High / (Hi)

Periodical House, Canton OH.

May 1957 – November 1959. 15 issues.

Fiction, nonfiction, pictorials.

This magazine started out (well, for one issue) as *Hi* with a companion title called *Ho!* Even stranger, both magazines were of the odd size 4 by 11 inches, probably to stand out from the competition. This experiment must have failed, because by the seventh issue (June 1958) it had assumed a more regular magazine size, and *Ho!* was gone completely.

High Adventure

'For men who dare.'

April – October 1959. 3 issues.

Adventure fiction.

High Heels

Selbee Associates Inc., New York NY; Consolidated Publishing.

1961 – 1970. 22 issues?

Pictorials.

This was of course a bit of a fetish magazine, not related to the related Eros title of the 70's.

At least 1 issue, #3, features the phrase 'Combined with *Stocking Parade*.'

High Time

American Art Agency Inc., Hollywood CA (Parliament).

1960 – 1969? 30+ issues.

Pictorials.

Highball

Comet Publications, Los Angeles CA.

1963 – 1966. ~15 issues.

Pictorials.

Hi-Living

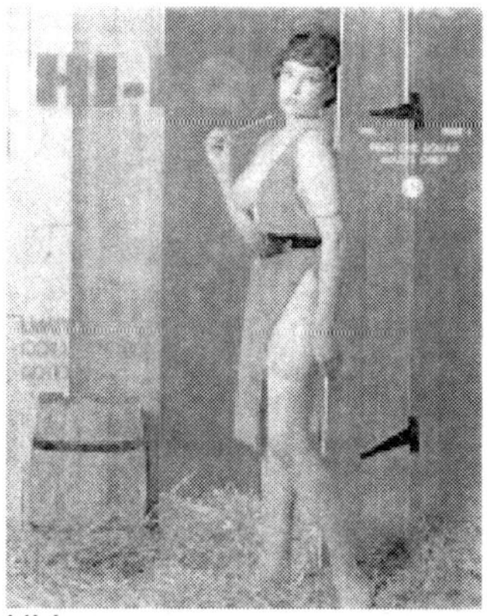
Hi-Lo

Hide and Seek

High

High

High Adventure

High Heels

High Time

Highball

Hip & Toe
Comet Publications, Beverly Hills CA.
1963 – ? At least 10-15 issues published.
Pictorials.

Hippy
Sari Publishing Co., North Hollywood CA.
Early 1960's. How many issues were published?
Pictorials.
Was there more than one magazine with this title?

His / His World
'A magazine for real men.'
Westridge Publishing.
February 1963 – August 1954? 6 issues?
Adventure fiction.
Apparently this was *His* for 2 issues before becoming *His World* for the last 4.

Hit
Volitant Publishing Corp., New York NY.
Black and white interiors.
March 1942 – 1959? 100+ issues.
Pictorials.

Hit Show
MDA Publishing Corp., New York NY.
March 1957 – 1961. ~20 issues.
Pictorials.

Ho!
See *High*.

Hollywood DreamGirl
Hollywood DreamGirl, New York NY.
Black and white interior.
1950's. One-shot.
Pictorials, nonfiction.
Despite the title, this magazine features photos of lots of different young women, not just Hollywood actresses.

Hollywood Glamor Girls
Berkley Publishing Corp., New York NY.
1958. One-shot?
The first (only?) issue was completely devoted to Anita Ekberg.

Hip and Toe

Hippy

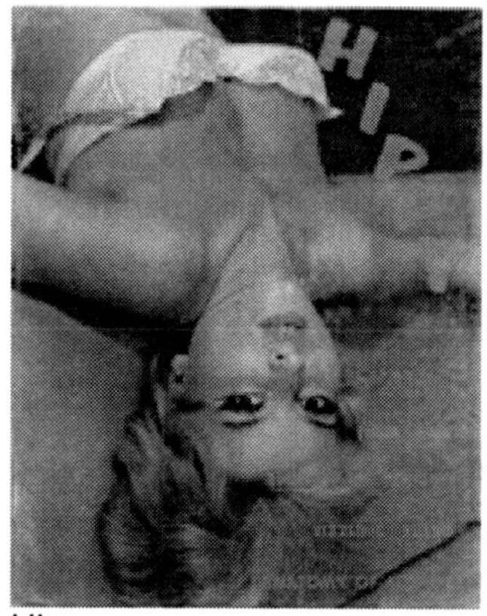
Hippy

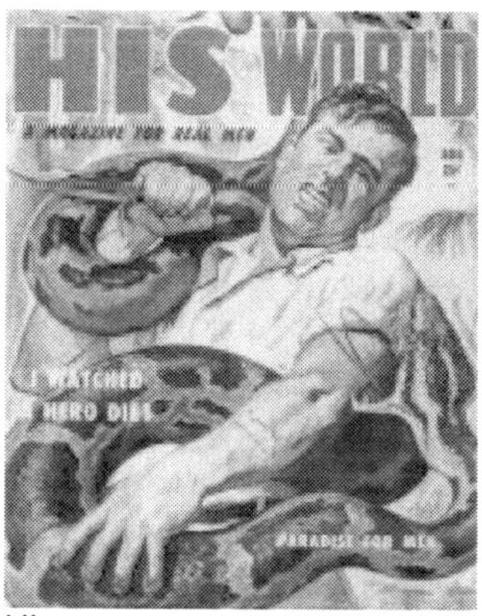

His

His

Hit

Hit

Hit Show

Hit Show

(Charlie Julian's) Hollywood Playgirls

Mid-1960's. How many issues were published?

There seems to have been more than one magazine of this period with this exact title, or at least two v.1 #1's.

Hollywood Playgirls

RNS Publications, Los Angeles CA.

1966. More than 1 issue published?

This appears to be a different publication from the previous entry.

Hollywood Sex Queens

1966. One-shot?

Hollywood Showtime

1960's. At least 3 issues produced?

Honey

American Art Agency Inc., Hollywood CA (Parliament).

1962 – 1965; 1968 – 1974. 30+ issues.

Pictorials.

The first incarnation of this title (both were Parliament books) featured the tame semi-nude photography available at the time, while the later version offered harder fare.

Honey Holiday

Late 1960's? One-shot.

This magazine appears to have been released with both $3.50 and $4.00 cover prices; the latter might have been during the early 1970's.

Note: This title features full, hardcore nude photos, of a single model.

Hot

Patra Publications, New York NY.

1960's. How many issues were published?

Hot Spot

American Art Agency Inc., Hollywood CA (Parliament).

1963 – 1964. 4 issues.

Pictorials.

How To Decorate A Bachelor's Apartment

1966. One-shot.

Pictorials.

This curious one-off basically showed various semi-nude women cleaning and spiffing up a home.

Hollywood Playgirls (1st)

Hollywood Playgirls (2nd)

Hollywood Sex Queens

Hollywood Showtime

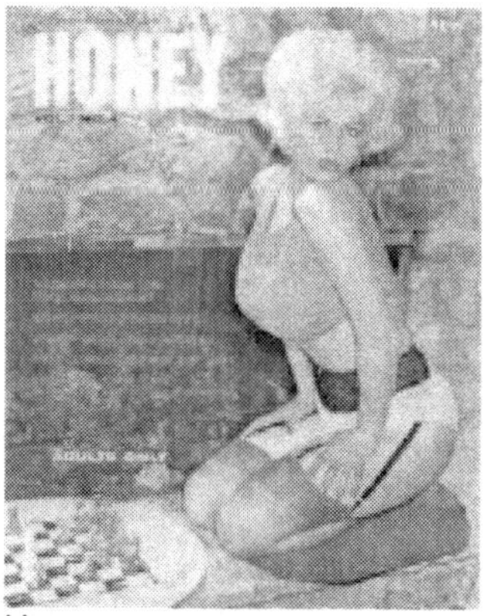

Honey

Honey

Honey Holiday

Hot Spot

How To Decorate...

HQ

See *Harlequin*.

Humorama

Humorama Inc., New York NY (Atlas).

Black and white interiors. Measures 5.5 by 7.5 inches.

1957 – 1963? 30+ issues?

Pictorials, cartoons.

Hunting Adventures

Newsstand Publications (Atlas), New York NY.

Fall 1954 – Spring 1957. 11 issues.

Adventure fiction.

Another of powerhouse Atlas's fiction mags for men, this time, as the title implies, focusing on outdoor and wildneress tales.

Imp

Sari Publishing Co., North Hollywood CA.

Black and white interiors, with color centerfolds.

Early 1960's. At least 3 issues.

Pictorials.

Impact

Macfadden Publications.

April – September 1953; 1964-1965. 12-15 issues?

Nonfiction, fiction, pictorials.

The first Macfadden incarnation of this title lasted only about 3 issues. The second, starting again in early 1964, seems to have been a (temporary?) retitling of the same publisher's *Climax*.

Impact

Hanro Corp., New York NY.

June 1957 – March 1958? 5 issues?

Adventure fiction.

This seems to have been a short-lived magazine that had nothing to do with the (earlier and later) Macfadden Publications title.

Inside

'Photos for men.'

Cape Magazine Management Corp., New York NY.

Measures 4 by 6 inches.

1954 – 1958? 30+ issues.

Nonfiction, pictorials.

Humorama

Humorama

Hunting Adventures

Hunting Adventures

Imp

Imp

Impact (Macfadden)

Impact (Hanro)

Impact (Hanro)

Instant Laughs
Humorama Inc., New York NY (Atlas).
Black and white interiors. Measures 5.5 by 7.5 inches.
1960's? How many issues?

Interlude
Sampson Publishing and Distribution Co., New York NY.
Black and white interiors, with some color.
March 1963 – ? At least 3 issues published.

Islander, The
'A magazine for the wanderer.'
February 1962 – ? More than 1 issue produced?

Jackpot
'The cad's home companion.'
Olympic Publishing.
January 1957 – September 1958. 3 issues?
Pictorials, nonfiction, fiction.

Jade
'A gem of male entertainment.'
Billingsley Publications, Hollywood CA.
1960 – 1961. 3 issues.
Pictorials, fiction, nonfiction.

Jade (2nd)
'The ultimate in magazine entertainment.'
1962 – 1963. 3 issues.

Jade (3rd)
June 1965. 1 issue only?

Jaguar
'For the man about town.'
American Art Agency Inc., Hollywood CA (Parliament).
1961. 2 issues.

Jaguar
'The magazine for the male animal.'
Jaguar Publications Inc., New York NY.
Black and white and color interiors.
December 1964 – 1979. 100+ issues, plus at least 5 large-size special issues.
Pictorials, nonfiction, fiction, cartoons.

Interlude

Islander

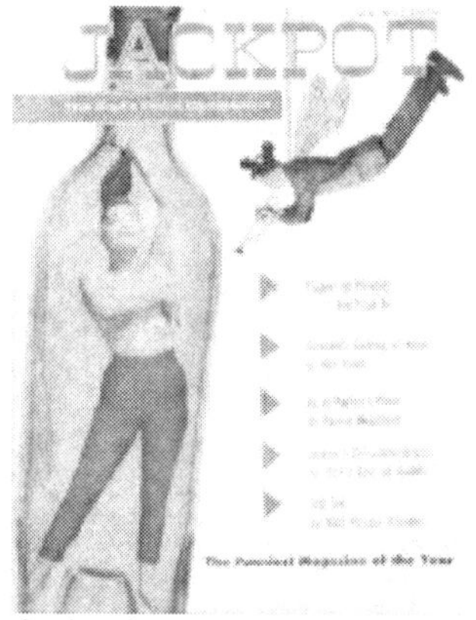

Jackpot

Jackpot

Jade (Billingsley)

Jade (1963)

Jaguar (1st)

Jaguar (1st)

Jaguar (2nd)

The Jayne Mansfield Pin-Up Book
1960's. One-shot.
Pictorials, nonfiction.

Jem
Body Beautiful Publications Inc., Jersey City NJ.
November 1956 – December 1967. 55 issues.
Pictorials, fiction, nonfiction, cartoons.
This title eventually became the purely pornographic title *Gem*.

Jest
Humorama Inc., New York NY (Atlas).
Black and white interiors. Measures 5.5 by 7.5 inches.
1948 – 1963? ~85 issues.
Cartoons, pictorials.

Jester
Art Enterprises Inc., Los Angeles CA.
'The ribald magazine.'
1960. 2 issues.
Pictorials, fiction, nonfiction.

Jigger
Franklin Publications, North Hollywood CA.
1964. More than 2 issues published?
Pictorials.

Joker
Humorama Inc., New York NY (Atlas).
Black and white interiors. Measures 5.5 by 7.5 inches.
1942 – 1976? 100+ issues.
Cartoons, pictorials.

Jolie
Delilah Publishing Corp., New York NY.
Black and white interiors.
1962. More than one issue exist?
Pictorials.

Joy
1959 – 1960? How many issues were published?
Pictorials.

Jayne Mansfield Pin-Up Book

Jem

Jem

Jest

Jest

Jester

Jigger

Joker

Joker

Joy
Delilah Publishing Corp., New York NY.
Black and white interiors.
1962. More than one issue exist?
Pictorials.

Jubilee (1st)
1950. More than 1 issue published?
Pictorials, nonfiction.
Was this simply v.1 #1 of the American Art Agency title from 1969?

Jubilee
American Art Agency Inc., Hollywood CA (Parliament).
Black and white interior, with color centerfold.
1962. More than 1 issue exist?
Pictorials, nonfiction.

Jubilee (3rd)
Black and white interior, with color centerfold.
1965. More than 1 issue exist?

Jubilee
American Art Agency Inc., Hollywood CA (Parliament).
1969. More than 2 issues published?
Pictorials.
Is this just a continuation of the 1962 title?

Jumbo Man's Magazine
Counterpoint, Inc., New York NY.
Early 1960's. One-shot?
Adventure fiction.
This was apparently two or more magazines rebound together. What titles?

Jump
1960's. How many issues published?

Kalendoscope '68
Elysium Inc., Hollywood CA (Parliament).
1968. Only 1 issue?
Pictorials.

Kandie
Tee Jay Publishing.
1960's.

Jolie

Joy (1959)

Joy (Delilah)

Jubilee (1950)

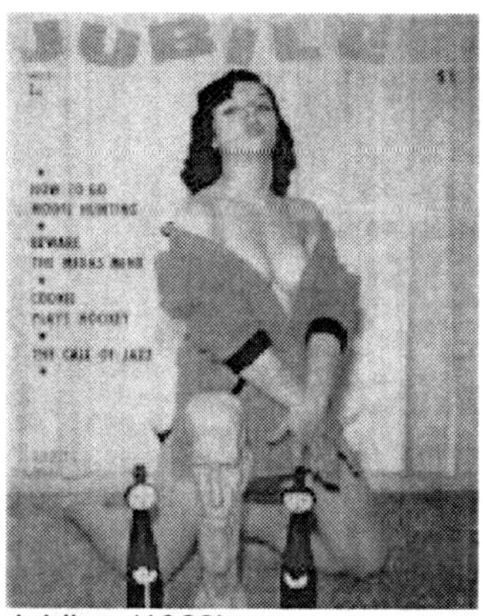

Jubilee (1962)

Jubilee (1969)

Kalendoscope 68

Kandie

Ken For Men

Ken For Men

Male Publishing, New York NY (Atlas).

June 1956 – 1961? 15 issues?

Adventure fiction.

This title too seems to have an odd history. There seems to be a stray v.4 #1 from 1961. Also, the August 1957 issue seems to have been titled *Complete Man's Magazine*. Atlas's later *Complete Man* apparently took over the numbering from this title, but the one doesn't otherwise seem to be a continuation.

Kick

Marst Publishing Co., North Hollywood CA (Seven Seventy?).

1961. More than 1 issue published?

Pictorials, nonfiction, fiction.

Kick

Dominion Publishing Co., Hollywood CA.

1968 – ? At least 2 issues.

Pictorials.

Kick

Seven Seventy Publishers, North Hollywood CA.

1960's. At least 6 issues published.

Pictorials.

Note that issues #5 and #6 were titled *Kick For Joy*.

Kick for Joy

See previous entry.

King

Sari Publishing Co., North Hollywood CA.

Fall 1958 – 1963. 7 issues, plus 2 larger special issues (Annual/Special).

Pictorials, fiction, nonfiction.

Not to be confused with the late-60's publication of the same name, nor the 70's British title.

Note: with the 8th issue, the title changed to *King's Man* (see next entry).

King's Man

Sari Publishing Co., North Hollywood CA.

1961 – 1966? 10+ issues?

Pictorials, fiction, nonfiction.

Kiss (1st)

'The world's most kissable girls.'

1962 – 1963? At least 2 issues, plus one Annual.

Pictorials, nonfiction.

Ken For Men

Ken For Men

Kick (Marst)

Kick (Dominion)

Kick (770)

King

King

King's Man

Kiss (1962)

Kiss

Comet Publications, Los Angeles CA.

1960's? At least 2 issues.

Issue #2 appears to be a complete reprint of the other *Kiss* title's first issue, with a new cover.

Kitten

'A magazine for meowing about.'

Triumph News Co., Van Nuys CA; Dominion Publishing Co., Hollywood CA.

1967 – 1969. ~10 issues.

Pictorials, nonfiction.

Knave

'Adult fun for men.'

Loki Publishing Co., White Plains NY.

January – December 1959. 6 issues.

Fiction, nonfiction, pictorials.

Note to be confused with at least 2 later pornographic publications.

Knight

Sirkay Publications, Los Angeles CA.

November 1962 – September 1978. 100+ issues.

Pictorials, nonfiction.

This title started out as *Sir Knight*; this later incarnation was a bit more sex-oriented, and as the late 60's rolled around turned more toward full nudity and eventually pornographic content.

La Belle

D. Collison Publications, Las Vegas NV.

1960. 4 issues published.

Pictorials, nonfiction, fiction.

Note: The 4th issue is a compilation issue, with several other magazines' interiors basically stapled together under the one cover. The cover price for this was $3.00 as opposed to previous (normal) issues costing $1.00.

Not to be confused with the title *La Belles* from the 1970's.

La Belle Femme

Sampson Publishing and Distribution Co., New York NY.

1960. Only 1 issue?

Pictorials, fiction.

La Femme

D. Collison Publications, Las Vegas NV.

1961. Only 1 issue?

Kiss (Comet)

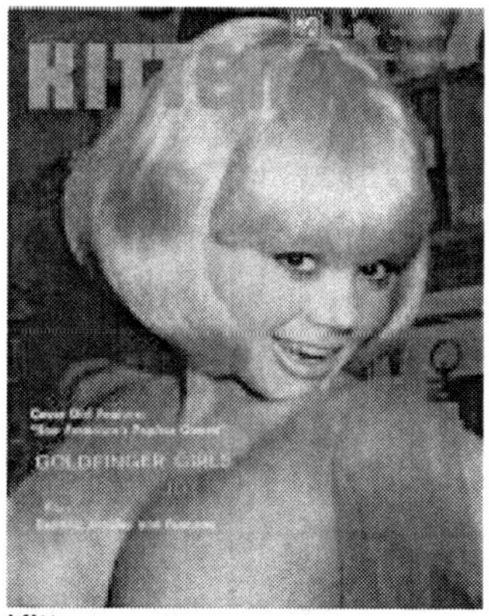

Kitten

Kitten

Knave

Knight

Knight

La Belle

La Belle Femme

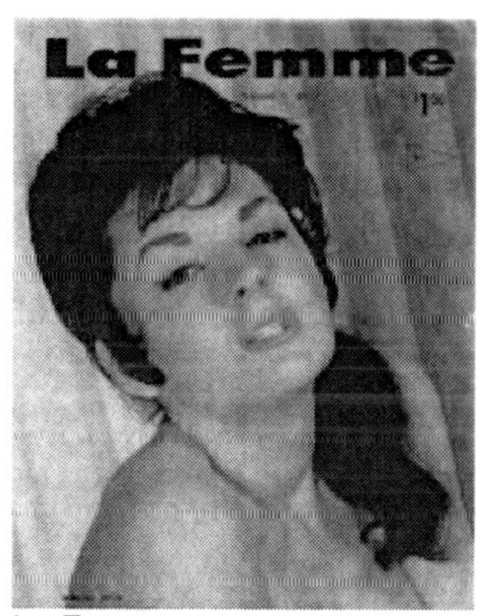

La Femme

Lace Undies
'The peek-a-boo magazine.'
Art Enterprises Inc., Los Angeles CA.
1960's. At least 3 issues published.

Lady Blue
Tuxedo Books Inc. Publishing, New York NY.
1960's. How many issues published?
Pictorials.

Laff
Volitant Publishing Corp., New York NY.
Measures 10.5 by 13.5 inches.
December 1939 – 1959? 100+ issues.
Nonfiction, humor, pictorials.

Laff
KMR Publications Inc., New York NY.
July – October 1965. More than 2 issues?
Humor, pictorials.
This was obviously a humor/parody mag, but also featured plenty of glamour photography.
This was previously *Laffboy* (see next entry).

Laffboy
KMR Publications, New York NY.
February – April 1965. 2 issues.
Nonfiction, humor, pictorials.
This was a parody of *Playboy* and magazines like it; the design was certainly closely copied after Hefner's work of the time.
With the 3rd issue, it became just *Laff* (see previous entry).

Lancer
'The best magazine for real men.'
September – November 1960. 2 issues.
Fiction, nonfiction, pictorials.

Lark (1st)
'Fun outdoors.'
Early 1960's? At least 2 issues.

Lark
Lark Magazine, New York NY.
1969. How many issues produced?

Lace Undies

Laff (Volitant)

Laff (Volitant)

Laff (KMR)

Laffboy

Laffboy

Lancer

Lark (1st)

Lark (1969)

Las Vegas Holiday
Samuel L. Sherman Publications, Los Angeles CA.
1962. Only 1 issue published?
Nonfiction, pictorials.

(Charlie Julian's) Las Vegas Party Girls
Las Vegas Playgirl Inc., Carson City NV.
Nonfiction, pictorials.

(Charlie Julian's) Las Vegas Playgirl
Las Vegas Playgirl Inc., Carson City NV.
August 1960 – March 1961. 3 issues published.
Nonfiction, pictorials.

Las Vegas Playground
February 1962 – ? How many issues were published?
Nonfiction, pictorials.

(Charlie Julian's) Las Vegas Showgirl
Charles A. Julian Enterprises, Las Vegas NV?
1962. More than 1 issue published?
Pictorials, nonfiction, cartoons.

(Charlie Julian's) Las Vegas Swings
Charles A. Julian Enterprises, Las Vegas NV.
Black and white interiors, with color centerfolds. Measures 8.5 by 10.75 inches.
1962. More than 1 issue published?
Pictorials, nonfiction.

Lasses & Glasses
American Art Agency., Hollywood CA (Parliament).
1968 – early 1970's? At least 6 issues.
Pictorials.

Late Date
American Art Agency / Jaybird Enterprises, Hollywood CA (Parliament).
1962 – 1973. 35+ issues.
Pictorials.

Late Show
American Art Agency Inc., Hollywood CA (Parliament).
May 1962 – 1973. 43 issues.
Pictorials, nonfiction.

Las Vegas Holiday

Las Vegas Party Girls

Las Vegas Playgirl

Las Vegas Showgirl

Las Vegas Swings

Late Date

Late Date

Late Show

Late Show

Latest Lovelies

N.M. Corp., New York NY.

1963. 2 issues published.

Pictorials.

(Charley Jones') Laugh Book Magazine

Charles Jones Publishing.

Black and white interiors. Measures 5 by 7 inches.

1945 – 1963? 100+ issues.

Cartoons, pictorials.

Laugh Circus

Humorama Inc., New York NY (Atlas).

Black and white interiors. Measures 5.5 by 7.5 inches.

1960's? How many issues?

Laugh Digest

Humorama Inc., New York NY (Atlas).

Black and white interiors. Measures 5.5 by 7.5 inches.

1962 – 1971? ~60 issues.

Cartoons, pictorials.

Confusingly, the numbering for this title apparently starts at #49 (or is it #48?) in 1962, going up to #81 before restarting with #4.

Laugh It Off

Humorama Inc., New York NY (Atlas).

Black and white interiors. Measures 5.5 by 7.5 inches.

1960 – 1961. 7 issues.

Cartoons, pictorials.

Laugh Riot

Humorama Inc., New York NY (Atlas).

Black and white interiors. Measures 5.5 by 7.5 inches.

1960 – 1966? ~40 issues.

Cartoons, pictorials.

Lavender & Lace

Walter Scott Publications, North Hollywood CA; Comet Publications, Beverly Hills CA.

1964 – 1967? How many issues published?

Pictorials.

Latest Lovelies

Latest Lovelies

Laugh Book

Laugh Digest

Laugh Digest

Laugh Riot

Laugh Riot

Lavender & Lace

Lavender & Lace

Leg-O-Rama

Batters Publications Inc., Hollywood CA.

Black and white interiors, with some color photos.

1959 – ? How many issues were produced?

Pictorials.

Obviously, with Elmer Batters being the publisher, this was a leg/nylon fetish title.

Leg Show

Selbee Associates Inc., New York NY.

1961 – 1965? ~10 issues.

Pictorials.

Leg World of Elmer Batters, The

Press Arts Inc., Canoga Park CA.

1967 – ? How many issues were published?

Pictorials.

Leg fetish mag.

Legs & Lasses

1960's. How many issues were published?

Pictorials, nonfiction, fiction.

Legs That Dance to Elmer's Tune

Press Arts Inc., Canoga Park CA.

1969. At least 3 issues.

Pictorials.

This title was also later given to a hardcover collection published by Taschen of Elmer Batters's fetish photography, in 1997.

Les Dames

American Art Agency Inc., Hollywood CA (Parliament).

1960's. At least 5 issues published.

Pictorials.

Les Starlettes

Sampson Publishing and Distribution Co., New York NY.

Early 1960's. More than 1 issue produced?

Pictorials.

Life Study

Camerarts Publishing Co., Chicago IL.

1955 – 1959? ~20 issues.

Pictorials.

Leg-O-Rama

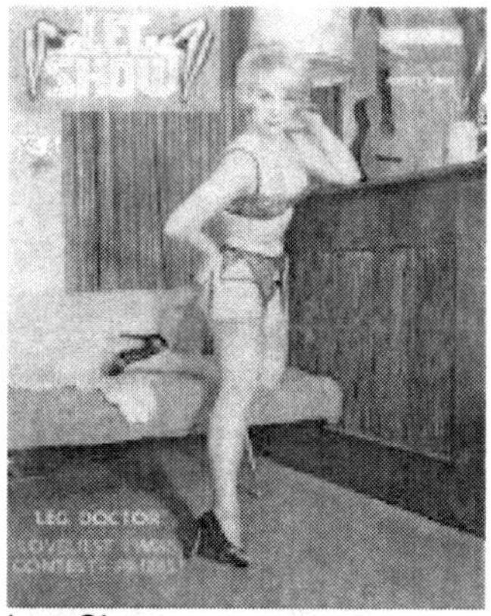

Leg Show

Leg Show

The Leg World Of...

Legs & Lasses

Legs That Dance To...

Les Dames

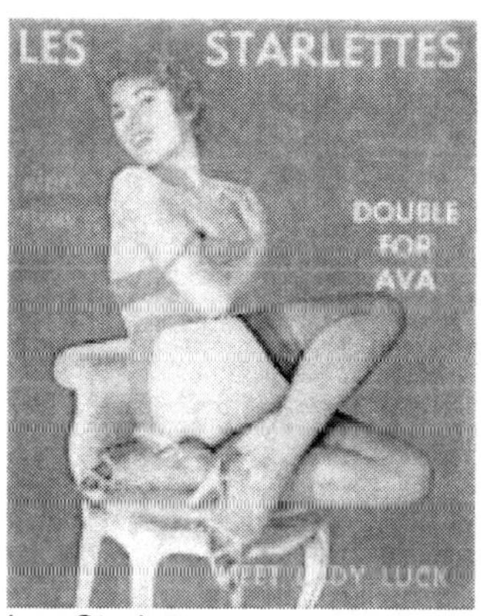

Les Starlettes

Life Study

Like Wild!
Bonanza Publishing Co., North Hollywood CA.
Black and white interiors, with additional colors and color centerfolds.
1960's. At least 2 issues produced.
Pictorials, nonfiction.

Line & Form
Jaybird Enterprises, Hollywood CA (Parliament).
1967 – 1978? 40+ issues.
Pictorials.

Lion Adventures
May – July 1960. More than 2 issues?
Adventure fiction.

Lithe
Sprite Publishing Co.
Black and white interiors, with color centerfolds.
Early 1960's? At least 2 issues published.
Pictorials.

Lonesome Gals
Press Arts Inc., Canoga Park CA.
1967 – 1970? At least 10 issues.
Pictorials.

Lovely
Black and white interiors, with some color photos.
1960's. At least 2 issues produced.
Pictorials.
Not to be confused with a Swedish import magazine from this era.

Lucky (For Men)
Agard Publishing.
1961. 3 issues published?
Nonfiction, fiction, pictorials.

Lucky
Triumph News Co. Inc., Van Nuys CA.
Late 1960's. How many issues produced?
Pictorials.

Like Wild!

Line and Form

Lion Adventures

Lithe

Lonesome Gals

Lovely

Lucky For Men (Agard)

Lucky For Men (Agard)

Lucky (Triumph)

Lure

Imperial Publishing Co., Hollywood CA.

Early 1960's. At least 3 issues?

Pictorials.

Luscious

Antony Publications Inc., New York NY.

1962 – 1965? 18 issues?

Pictorials.

Not to be confused with similarly-titled mags from the 1980's and the 1990's.

Lusty

Bonanza Publishing Co., North Hollywood CA.

Black and white interiors, with color centerfolds.

1963. More than 1 issue published?

Pictorials, fiction.

Lusty

Seven Seventy Publishers, North Hollywood CA.

1966. How many issues published?

Lusty

Mecca Magazines, Sherman Oaks CA.

July 1969 - ? How many issues were produced?

Pictorials.

Madcap

American Art Agency Inc., Hollywood CA (Parliament).

1962 – 1966. 13 issues?

Pictorials.

Magnifique

Sampson Publishing and Distribution Co., New York NY.

Late 1950's? (No date given.) Only 1 issue published, apparently.

Pictorials.

Male

Atlas Magazines Inc. (under various publisher names), New York NY.

June 1950 – 1981? 100+ issues, plus Annuals.

Primarily fiction, also pictorials and nonfiction.

Throughout most of its run, *Male* was the very definition of the men's adventure fiction magazine. It later devolved into a straight men's nudie title; this can be seen starting in 1968-69 when the gorgeous painted covers started giving way to photographs.

Luscious

Lusty (770)

Madcap

Madcap

Magnifique

Male

Male

Male

Male

Male Call

1965. Only 1 issue published?

Pictorials.

Not to be confused with the in-house military magazine for servicemen, nor the slightly later gay porn title.

Male Life

Magnum Publications Inc., New York NY.

Measures 4 by 6 inches.

May 1955 – January 1957. 19 issues.

Pictorials.

Bettie Page graces the cover of June 1955.

Male Point of View

Point Magazines Inc., Atlanta GA.

Black and white interiors. Measures 4 by 6 inches.

October 1955 – October 1958. 30+ issues.

Nonfiction, pictorials.

This magazine was actually titled *Point* from its first issue (March 1954) to September 1955; and the title was changed again to *Man's Point of View* starting with the April 1959 number until it ceased publication ca. 1963.

Note: The February 1956 cover features a delectable Marilyn Monroe, making this issue usually quite a bit more expensive than others.

Mamas, The

Triumph News Co. Inc., Van Nuys CA.

1960's. How many issues were produced?

Pictorials.

Man About Town

Lucky Magazines, New York NY.

September 1958 – ? How many issues were published?

Fiction, nonfiction, pictorials, cartoons.

Man to Man

Picture Magazines, Inc., New York NY; Volitant Publishing Corp., New York NY.

December-January 1949 – 1982? 100+ issues, plus giant-sized special issues.

Fiction, nonfiction, pictorials.

This title was around so long that it started out with an emphasis on semi-nude photospreads, made the transition to men's adventure fiction, then came back around to (by the 1970's) full-nudity photospreads.

Manhood

International Publications Inc., Hollywood CA.

1962 – 1963. 6 issues.

Pictorials, nonfiction.

Male Call

Male Life

Male Point of View

Man About Town

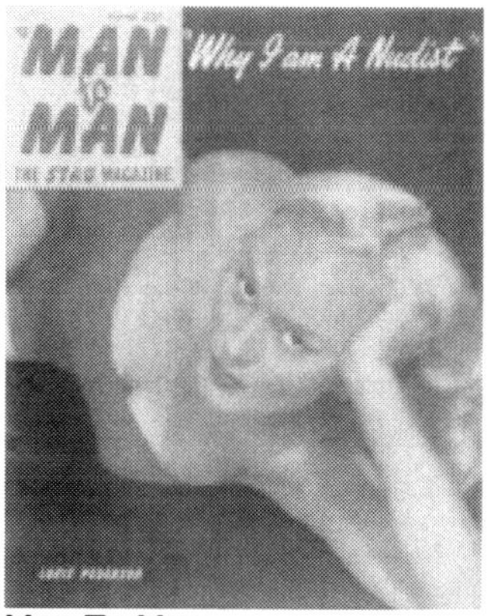

Man To Man

Man To Man

Man To Man

Manhood

Manhood

Man's Action

Candar Publishing Co. Inc., New York NY.

June 1957 – 1977? 100+ issues?

Adventure fiction with nonfiction, pictorials, and cartoons.

Man's Adventure

Stanley Publications, New York NY.

May 1957 – 1971? ~100 issues.

Adventure fiction, pictorials, nonfiction.

For most of its lifetime this was a straight men's adventure fiction magazine with the usual painted covers; then in late 1967, for a short time, it became a regular girlie pictorial mag with photo covers, as most titles were trending at the time. It reappeared again briefly in 1971 again focusing on fiction & nonfiction.

Man's Age

AAA Magazines Inc., New York NY.

May 1962 – December 1962. 4 issues.

Adventure fiction.

Man's Best

Normandy Associates, New York NY (Stanley).

September 1961 – March 1967. 18 issues?

Adventure fiction.

This title seems to have taken a few years off between mid-1963 and 1966, for some reason.

Man's Book

Reese Publishing Co., Inc.; EmTee Publishing, New York NY.

March 1962 – 1974? 72 issues?

Adventure fiction.

This title has a lot of Nazi covers during the mid-60's.

Man's Cavalcade

Skye Publishing Co., Inc., New York NY.

April 1957 – January 1958. 4 issues.

Adventure fiction.

This title became simply *Cavalcade* with its fifth issue in March 1958.

Man's Combat

Garnet Publications Inc., Derby CT.

June 1969 – Autumn 1970. 6 issues.

Adventure fiction.

Man's Action

Man's Action

Man's Adventure

Man's Adventure

Man's Best

Man's Book

Man's Book

Man's Cavalcade

Man's Combat

Man's Conquest

Hanro Corp., New York NY; QMG Magazines.

April 1955 – April 1972. 100+ issues.

Adventure fiction.

The covers to this title were especially masculine and rugged. Part of the cover image for the August 1958 issue was used for the cover of Feral House's *It's A Man's World*.

The first issue was called simply *Conquest*.

Man's Courage

1963. 1 issue?

Adventure fiction, pictorials?

Man's Daring

Candar Publishing Co., Inc., New York NY.

June 1959 – December 1966. 43 issues.

Adventure fiction.

This title became just *Daring*, a straight-up girlie photo mag, starting with v.7 #4, February 1967. The first 3 issues were called *Man's Daring Action*.

Man's Daring Action

See *Man's Daring*.

Man's Daring Adventures

Star Publications, Inc.

November 1955 – October 1956. 4 issues.

Adventure fiction, nonfiction.

Man's Day

Hillman Periodicals Inc., New York NY.

August 1952 – August 1953; December 1960 – April-May 1961. 10 issues.

Adventure fiction & nonfiction.

This magazine lasted only 7 issues in its initial early run, then came back for a very short time in 1960.

Man's Epic

EmTee Publishing, New York NY.

September 1963 – October 1973. ~61 issues.

Adventure fiction, nonfiction, pictorials.

Note that there was an Australian magazine called *Man's Epic* that is not to be confused with this one.

Man's Era

AAA Magazines Inc., New York NY.

June 1963. Only 1 issue?

Adventure fiction.

Man's Conquest

Man's Conquest

Man's Daring

Man's Daring

Man's Daring Adventures

Man's Day

Man's Day

Man's Epic

Man's Epic

Man's Escape

Pontiac Publishing.

April 1963 – February 1964. 6 issues.

Adventure fiction.

Man's Exploits

'For men who dare to live.'

Arnold Magazines Inc., Stamford CT.

June 1957 – April 1958; February 1963 – March 1964. 11 issues?

Adventure fiction.

Started by Everett M. 'Busy' Arnold, the same who had been responsible for the Quality Comics line that introduced such characters as Plastic Man and the Blackhawks, this title took a five-year hiatus for some reason.

Man's Fate

November 1962 – January 1963. 2 issues.

Adventure fiction.

Man's Favorite Pastime

Kelly Publishing Co., Long Beach CA; Rilgac Publishing Co., Hollywood CA; etc .

1958 – 1971? 40+ issues?

Without having access to a sizable collection of this title, it seems nearly impossible to determine which numbers were issued, or when, or under what publisher names. There seem to be multiple issues of v.1 #3, for example, from 1960-1961. Also, one can find issues under at least half a different publisher names – and while many of these will turn out to be the same publisher under different names, at this point it's just too big a mess to wade through without more information being available.

Man's Funtime

1961. More than 1 issue published?

Pictorials, nonfiction, fiction.

Man's Hour

AAA Magazines Inc., New York NY.

November 1963 – January 1964. 2 issues.

Adventure fiction.

Man's Illustrated

Hanro Corp.; QMG Magazine Corp.

July 1955 – April 1975. 100+ issues.

Adventure fiction, nonfiction, pictorials.

Man's Life

Crestwood; Stanley Publications, New York NY.

November 1952 – 1975? 100+ issues, plus at least 1 Annual.

Fiction, nonfiction, pictorials.

Man's Escape

Man's Exploits

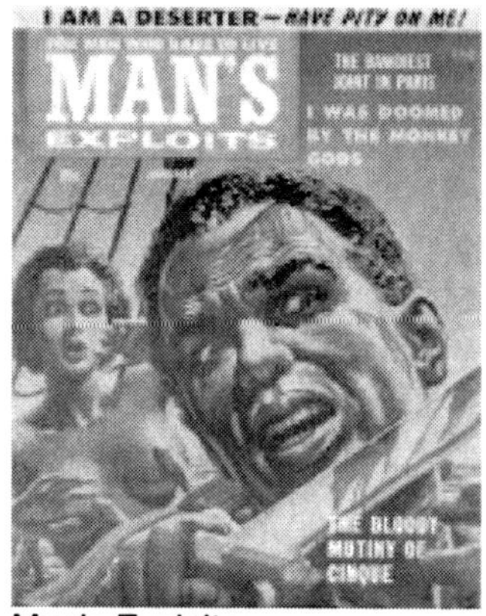

Man's Exploits

Man's Favorite Pastime

Man's Funtime

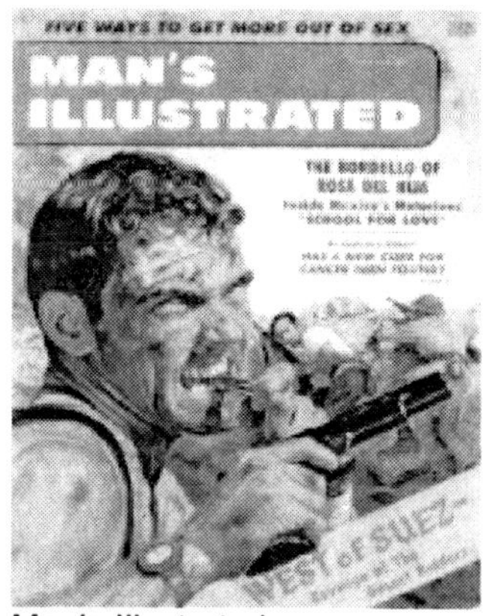

Man's Illustrated

Man's Illustrated

Man's Life

Man's Life

Although it later devolved into a more traditional girlie mag, this title started out as one of the great men's adventure fiction mags. Early covers were beautifully painted, usually showing a tense scene of man vs. nature; for example, the infamous 'Weasels Ripped My Flesh' cover, which inspired the Frank Zappa song title, was on the September 1956 issue.

Man's Look

Normandy Associates, New York NY (Stanley).

August 1961 – February 1962. 4 issues.

Fiction and nonfiction.

Man's Magazine

Pyramid Publications (under a handful of publisher names).

October 1952 – 1976? 100+ issues, including several Annuals.

Fiction, nonfiction, pictorials.

This is another publication that was around so long that its contents morphed from one emphasis to another; like most men's magazines, it concentrated on adventure fiction early on, eventually becoming a girlie magazine late in life.

Man's Odyssey

January – March 1958. 2 issues.

Adventure fiction, nonfiction.

Man's Peril

Periodical Packagers; Natlus; Starbright.

May 1963 – March 1967. 20 issues.

Adventure fiction, nonfiction, pictorials.

This was a retitling of *Peril*.

Man's Pleasure

Stanley Publications Inc., New York NY.

1961 – 1962; 1968 – 1978? 60+ issues.

Pictorials, nonfiction.

This title seems to have had an unusual publshing history. The first two issues appeared in 1961 and 1962, respectively; then the magazine seems to have disappeared until reappearing again in 1968, where it was published irregularly through at least 1978.

Man's Point of View

Point Magazines Inc., Atlanta GA.

Black and white interiors. Measures 4 by 6 inches.

April 1959 – January 1963. ~20 issues.

Nonfiction, pictorials.

This magazine's title was originally *Point* and then *Male Point of View*.

Man's Look

Man's Magazine

Man's Magazine

Man's Odyssey

Man's Peril

Man's Peril

Man's Pleasure

Man's Pleasure

Man's Point Of View

Man's Power

AAA Magazines Inc., New York NY.

February – April 1963? 2 issues?

Adventure fiction.

Man's Prime

Normandy Associates, New York NY (Stanley).

July 1963 – March 1967? 22 issues?

Adventure fiction, nonfiction, pictorials.

Most, if not all, covers of this title featured a bound woman being threatened. The interior wasn't nearly so concentrated, thankfully.

Man's Smashing Stories

Reese Publishing Co., New York NY.

June – September 1959.

Adventure fiction.

Man's Story

Reese Publishing Co., New York NY; EmTee Publishing, New York NY.

February 1960 – December 1975? 100+ issues.

Adventure fiction, nonfiction, pictorials.

A *lot* of this magazine's covers featured Nazis and/or women being bound and threatened.

Man's Thrills

Magazine Management Corp., New York NY (Atlas).

January – October 1961. 4 issues.

Fiction, nonfiction, pictorials.

Man's Time

AAA Magazines Inc., New York NY.

1962. Only 2 issues published?

Adventure fiction.

Man's True Action

Star Editions (Star Publications), New York NY.

October 1955 – September 1956. 4 issues.

Adventure fiction.

Man's True Danger

Candar Publishing Co., New York NY; Major Magazines Corp., Sparta IL.

June 1962 – February 1972. 54 issues.

Fiction, nonfiction, pictorials.

Note: this may appear to be titled simply *True Danger* on many covers, but this is the correct title.

Man's Power

Man's Prime

Man's Smashing Stories

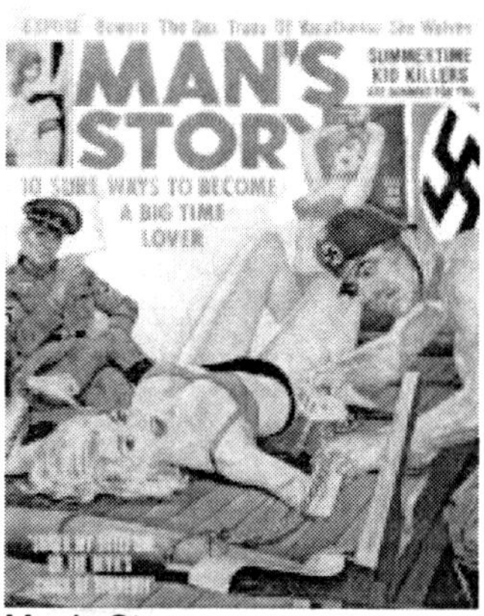

Man's Story

Man's Story

Man's Thrills

Man's Time

Man's True Danger

Man's True Danger

Man's Way

Magnum Publications Inc., New York NY.

Black and white interiors. Measures 4 by 6 inches.

March 1956 – 1957. ~10 issues.

Fiction, pictorials, nonfiction.

Man's Western

MTB Publications, New York NY.

1958 – 1959. 2 issues known.

Fiction, nonfiction, pictorials.

This title certainly counts as a 'men's magazine' rather than just a genre fiction magazine due to the fact that it had (clothed) female pictorials.

Man's World

Atlas Magazines Inc., New York NY (under various publisher imprints).

January 1951? – 1978? 100+ issues.

Fiction, nonfiction, pictorials.

The early publishing history of this title is a bit confusing. There seems to have been a couple of magazines appearing under this title in both 1951 and 1953, which may have been trial runs. But the title indisputably got underway (with v.1, #4) in December of 1955 as a men's adventure fiction magazine. It would continue thus, with the same high quality as Atlas's other similar titles, until about 1970, when it began featuring photo covers and started emphasizing the nude female photographs.

Note: The Dec. 1955 issue is v.1, #4; it took over the numbering of *Men in Action*.

Masher

Caesar Publishers Inc., New York NY.

1960's. How many issues?

Pictorials.

Master Photography

Arnold Magazines Inc., Stamford CT.

Summer – Winter 1957. 3 issues.

Pictorials, nonfiction.

Was this a photography mag that snuck in nudes, or a nudie mag that discussed photography?

Mate

Dominion Publishing Co., North Hollywood CA.

1960's. At least 3 issues.

Pictorials, fiction, nonfiction.

Mate! For Men

March 1961. One-shot?

Fiction & pictorials?

Man's Way

Man's Western

Man's World

Man's World

Man's World

Man's World

Man's World

Masher

Mate! For Men

Matinee

American Art Agency Inc., Hollywood CA (Parliament).

1962 – 1973? 30+ issues?

Pictorials.

Maverick

1969. At least 2 issues.

Nonfiction, pictorials.

Men

Atlas Magazines Inc., New York NY (under various publisher imprints).

March 1952 – 1982? 100+ issues, with several Annuals.

Adventure fiction, nonfiction, pictorials, cartoons.

This magazine also made the transition from men's fiction mag to girlie mag, with painted covers giving way to photos of beautiful women.

Men in Action

Medallion Publishing, New York NY (Atlas).

March – September 1955. 3 issues.

Adventure fiction.

This title changes to *Man's World* with the fourth issue.

Men in Adventure

Skye Publishing Co., New York NY.

May 1959 – December 1960. 9 issues.

Adventure fiction, nonfiction.

This title apparently continued (with v.2 #3) as *Bachelor*.

Note: There was another magazine with this title that started in 1963.

Men in Adventure

Jalart House, New York NY; Rostam Publications Inc., New York NY.

1963 – 1974? 50+ issues, plus at least 3 Annuals.

Fiction, nonfiction, pictorials.

The publishing history of this second version of this title isn't yet fully known. It *may* have started in 1963 with v.2 #3, taking over the numbering from the previous *Men in Adventure*; but it appears that a couple of issues going back to 1961 may have been found, also. Until we can find and document more issues, this will remain an open question.

Men in Combat

Hanro Corp., New York NY.

January 1957 – September 1957. 5 issues.

Adventure fiction.

This was retitled *Showdown for Men* with its sixth issue.

Matinee

Men

Men

Men

Men In Action

Men In Action

Men In Adventure

Men In Combat

Men In Combat

Men in Conflict

Normandy Associates, New York NY; Stanley Publications.

August 1961 – June 1963; April 1965 – March 1967. 28 issues?

Adventure fiction, nonfiction.

This title seems to have taken a hiatus during 1964, for whatever reason.

Men in Danger

Jalart House, New York NY.

January 1964 – April 1965. 6 issues.

Adventure fiction.

Men Today

Reese Publishing Co., New York NY; EmTee Publishing, New York NY.

April 1961 – 1976? ~95 issues.

Adventure fiction, nonfiction.

A large number of this title's covers featured women in bondage.

Men's Digest

Novel Books Inc., Chicago IL.

June 1957 – 1977. 150+ issues.

Nonfiction, pictorials, fiction, cartoons.

Men's Pictorial

New Publications.

February 1956 – February 1958. 13 issues.

Adventure fiction.

This title continues the numbering of a previous pulp magazine, *Fifteen Western Tales.*

Mermaid

Garden of Eve Publications Inc., New York NY.

Black and white interiors.

1958 – 1960. 16 regular issues plus 2 Annuals.

Fiction, pictorials, nonfiction.

Not to be confused with the *Mermaid* that started up a few years later (see next entry); you can usually tell the two apart by the cover logo font (see thumbnail scans).

Mermaid

Geemil Publications Inc., New York NY.

Black and white interiors with color centerfolds.

May 1962 – 1963. 6 issues.

Pictorials, fiction, nonfiction.

Men In Conflict

Men In Danger

Men Today

Men Today

Men's Digest

Men's Digest

Men's Pictorial

Mermaid (1958)

Mermaid (1962)

Midnight

American Art Agency Inc., Hollywood CA; Jaybird Enterprises, North Hollywood CA (Parliament).

Black and white with a few color photos, including centerfold.

1960 – 1970? 30+ issues.

Pictorials, fiction, nonfiction, cartoons.

Like most Parliament publications, this one was heavy on the nude photography but a bit light on the text features.

Millionaire

Millionaire Publications Inc., Long Beach CA.

March 1964 – 1966? 10+ issues.

Fiction, nonfiction, pictorials.

This magazine was devoted to a somewhat older, more affluent male reader.

Minx

Tri-S Publications, Hollywood CA.

Black and white with some color photos.

1959 – 1963. 6 issues.

Pictorials.

Minx (2nd)

Seven Seventy Publishers, North Hollywood CA.

1965. More than 1 issue published?

Pictorials.

Mister Cool

See *Mr. Cool*.

Mister Twenty-One

Monogram Publications, Los Angeles CA.

1961. Apparently only 1 issue published.

Pictorials, nonfiction.

Mistress

Walter Scott Publications, North Hollywood CA.

Black and white with color centerfold.

1964 – ? At least 4 issues produced.

Pictorials, fiction.

Misty

Caesar Publishers Inc., New York NY.

1962 – 1964? At least 4 issues.

Pictorials.

Midnight

Midnight

Millionaire

Millionaire

Minx (Tri S)

Minx (770)

Mister Twenty-One

Mistress

Misty

Model, The

'For figure and pinup photographers.' 'For the artists and sculpturers.'

Ridge Press.

1950's. At least 2 issues published.

Pictorials.

Yes, it does say 'sculpturers.'

Model Studies Annual

Amateur Art and Camera Magazine, New York NY.

1951 – 1961? ~15 issues.

Pictorials.

Modelette

Camerarts Publishing Co., Chicago IL.

'Model studies for artists.'

1958 – 1962. 14 issues plus 1 Annual.

Pictorials.

Models' Scrapbook

American Art Agency Inc., Hollywood CA.

1963 – ? Was more than 1 issue released?

Pictorials.

Modern Life Illustrated

Health Knowledge Inc., New York NY.

1960's. At least 2 issues produced.

Pictorials, nonfiction.

Modern Man

Publishers Development Corp., Skokie IL.

Black and white with some color photographs.

July 1951 – December 1976?. 300+ issues, plus quarterly/yearly Specials.

Nonfiction, pictorials, fiction, cartoons.

This long-running monthly title published plenty of adventure-oriented nonfiction stories as well as plenty of black and white pictorials, with color centerfolds and a few more color photos mixed in.

Modern Man Annual/Quarterly

Publishers Development Corp., Skokie IL.

1952 – 1977? 100 issues?

Nonfiction, pictorials, fiction, cartoons.

This was sort of an adjunct title to the regular-issue *Modern Man*.

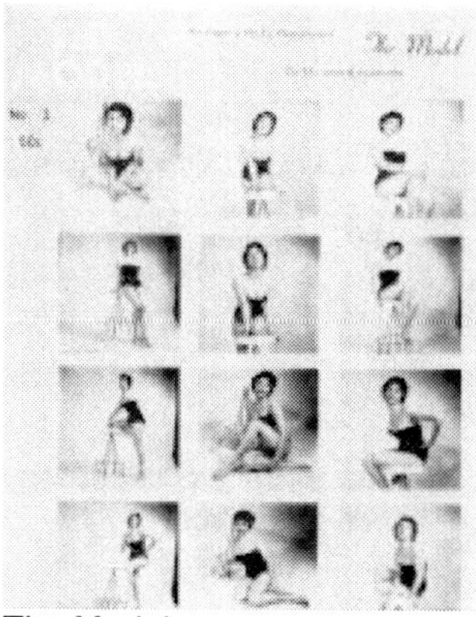

The Model

Model Studies Annual

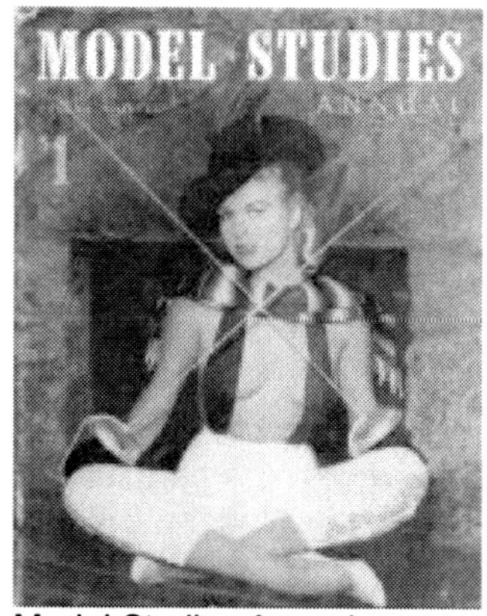

Model Studies Annual

Modelette

Modern Life

Modern Man

Modern Man

Modern Man Quarterly

Modern Man Quarterly

Mondo Freudo

New Link Publications, Hollywood CA.

Black and white, and duotone photos.

1966. One-shot.

Nonfiction, pictorials.

This was a one-shot magazine devoted to the subjects in the infamous *mondo* film. Like the movie, it skirts the edges of pornography but doesn't quite cross over.

Mondo Girls

1960's. At least 2 issues.

Pictorials.

There appears to be 2 different magazines from this era with this title, as there are apparently two different issues with different cover designs, each bearing 'Vol. 1 #1' on the cover.

Monsieur

Monsieur Publications, Union City NJ.

Black and white and color interiors.

February 1957 – March 1968. 57 issues.

Nonfiction, fiction, pictorials.

The color foldout photospreads curiously came at the front of some issues of this magazine, rather than in the center as with most titles (thus the term 'centerfold').

Mood

American Art Agency Inc., Hollywood CA.

1962 – 1964. 4 issues.

Pictorials.

Moonglow

American Art Agency Inc., Hollywood CA.

1962 – 1965. 5 issues.

Pictorials, nonfiction.

Note: The third issue of this title (v.1 #3) is incorrectly listed as v.1 #2 on the cover. (The correct v.1 #2 features the title in white letters, and a woman in red panties standing in front of a green wall; v.1 #3 has a red title against a black background, with a woman sitting.)

In addition to four regular-sized issues, there is also, oddly enough, an issue numbered #4 on the cover, but which appears to be an omnibus collection holding probably three other magazines rebound with a single cover. The contents of this issue may therefore vary from example to example.

Mosaic

Mosaic Productions, Los Angeles CA.

1961 – ? 5+ issues, plus at least 1 Annual.

Pictorials, nonfiction.

Mondo Girls

Monsieur

Monsieur

Monsieur

Mood

Moonglow

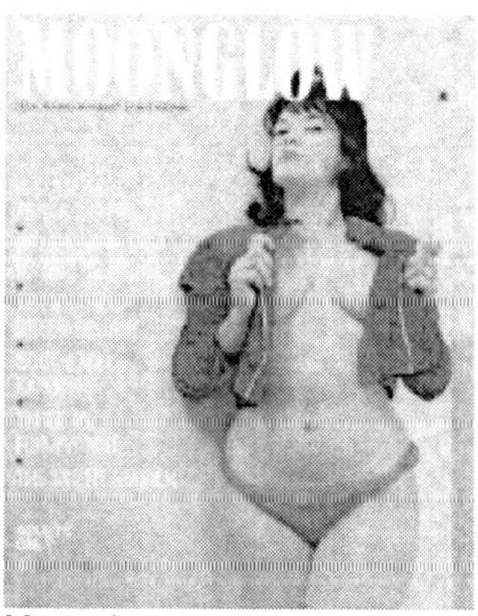
Moonglow

Mosaic

Mosaic

The Most

Minoan Publishing Corp.

1955. More than 2 issues?

Humor, cartoons, pictorials.

Minoan Publishing Corporation was apparently an imprint of Toby Press (or vice-versa), a company that produced comic books in the 1940's and early 1950's. Other humor titles published under the Minoan moniker (though not necessarily ones that fit into this volume) include *A-Laugh-A-Minnit* and *Bust Out Laffin'*.

Movie Pin-Ups

Ideal Publishing Corp., New York NY.

1951 – 1953. 5 issues.

Marilyn Monroe appeared on the March 1952 cover.

Mr.

Mr. Magazines Inc., New York NY.

Black and white interiors.

March 1950 – May 1954. 25 issues.

Nonfiction, pictorials.

Mr.

Counterpoint Inc., New York NY.

Color interiors.

July 1956 – August 1984. 200+ issues, including Annuals.

Pictorials, fiction, nonfiction, cartoons.

This second magazine under this title put its main emphasis on its color nude pictorials.

Mr. America

'For the man with a future.'

Weider Publications, Jersey City NJ.

August 1952 – August 1953. 10 issues.

Adventure fiction.

This brief title has an odd and interesting publishing history. For much of its lifetime, *Mr. America* was a bodybuilding/men's fitness magazine; then with the August 1952 issue (v.17 #5), it switched formats to men's adventure fiction, continuing this format monthly to the end of the year (and continuing to feature very toned, muscular men illustrated on the covers). With 1953, it split into two titles – *American Manhood* ('The Virile Magazine,' continuing with the cut young men on the covers) continuing the numbering, and *Mr. America* restarting with v.1, #1, but continuing only through August. Both titles apparently featured adventure fiction.

Mr. Cool

Billingsley Publications, Hollywood CA.

1960 – 1963? 4-6 issues?

Fiction, pictorials.

Note: This title is differentiated from the next ones by having the distributor initials 'GW' on the covers.

The Most

Movie Pin-Ups

Mr. (1950)

Mr. (1956)

Mr. (1956)

Mr. (1956)

Mr. America

Mr. America

Mr. Cool (Billingsley)

Mr. Cool
Roena Publications, Los Angeles CA.
1960. 1-3 issues?
Nonfiction, pictorials.
Issues from this publisher are differentiated by having the distributor initials 'FB' on the cover.

Mr. Cool
Ajax Publishing Co., Los Angeles CA.
1960's. More than 1 issue exist?
Pictorials.
Was this a continuation of one of the previous two titles?

The Mrs.
Press Arts Inc., Canoga Park CA.
Black and white interiors, with color centerfolds.
1960's. At least 6 issues.
Pictorials.

My Escort
Seeger Publications.
Black and white interiors, with color centerfolds.
1959. At least 3 issues.
Pictorials.

Mystic
Delilah Publishing & Distribution Co. Inc., New York NY.
Black and white with color centerfold.
Unknown date, but probably mid-to-late 1950's. More than one issue produced?
Pictorials, nonfiction, cartoons.
This mag was kind of done on the cheap, judging by its looks.

Mystique
Sari Publishing Co., North Hollywood CA.
1961 – ? At least 3 issues published.
Pictorials.
There are two #2's, although one (showing a young Asian woman) is designated as a 'special issue' on the cover.

Naughty Nylons
Sari Publishing Co., North Hollywood CA.
1962 – 1963? More than 2 issues published?
Pictorials.

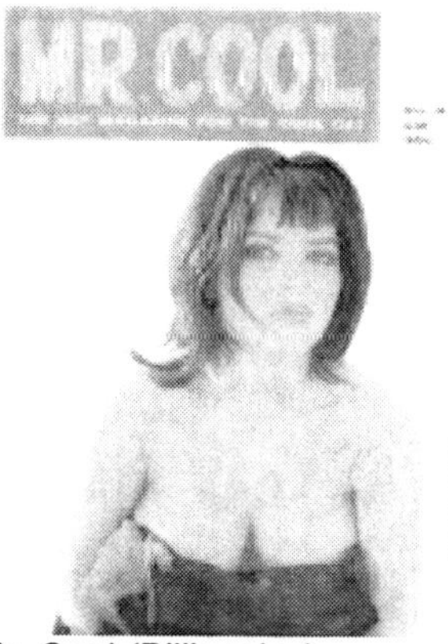

Mr. Cool (Billingsley)

Mr. Cool (Roena)

Mr. Cool (Ajax)

The Mrs.

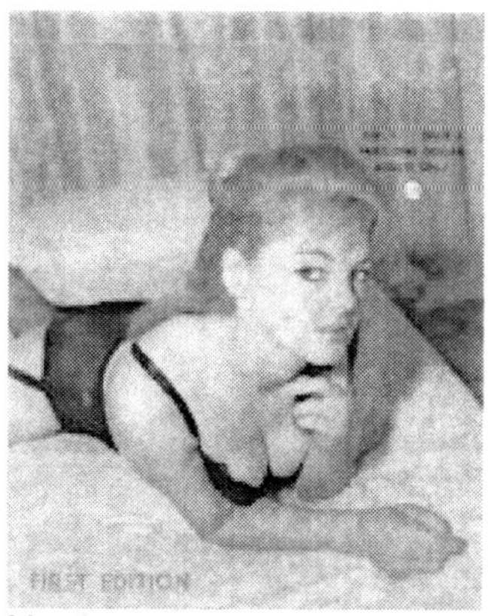

Mystic

Mystique

Mystique

Naughty Nylons

Naughty Nylons

Nectar
'For men with elegant taste.'
Early 1960's. More than 1 issue published?
Nonfiction, pictorials.

New Man
Reese Publishing Co., New York NY; EmTee Publishing, New York NY.
April 1963 – 1972? 55 issues?
Adventure fiction, nonfiction, pictorials.
Lots of Nazis and women being bound and threatened with torture on this title's covers.

Nifties
Health Knowledge Inc., New York NY.
1966 – 1971? At least 15 issues published.
Pictorials.

Nifty Nylons
Seven Seventy Publishers, North Hollywood CA.
1960's. At least 6 issues published.
Pictorials.
This magazine featured the cover title of *Classy Nifty Nylons* for its last few issues, apparently.

Night and Day
'America's picture magazine of entertainment.'
Alho Publishing Co., Mount Morris IL.
Black and white interiors. Measures 10 by 13 inches.
November 1948 – 1959. 100+ issues.
Nonfiction, pictorials.

Night and Day
Press Arts Inc., Canoga Park CA.
1964 – 1980? 100+ issues.
Pictorials.
This second incarnation of this title was certainly more overtly pornographic than the original tabloid.

Night-Life
Antony Publications Inc., New York NY.
Black and white interiors, with color centerfolds.
1960's. How many issues were published?

Nectar

New Man

Nifties

Nifty Nylons

Night and Day (1948)

Night and Day (1948)

Night and Day (1964)

Night and Day (1964)

Night Life

Night Out

Comet Publications, Los Angeles CA.

1963 – 1967? At least 11 issues published.

Pictorials.

Nightcap

Comet Publications, Los Angeles CA.

1960 – 1970's. How many issues were published?

Pictorials.

There seems to have been a gap of a few years from the mid-60's to the early 70's when this title wasn't published. It's not known quite where the numbering picked back up correctly.

Nightline

American Art Agency Inc., Hollywood CA.

Late 1960's – early 1970's. At least 14 issues published.

Pictorials.

Nite Out

Comet Publications, Los Angeles CA.

1963 – 1967. ~20 issues.

Pictorials.

Nite'ee

1960's. How many issues produced?

Nocturne

Selbee Associates Inc., New York NY.

1961 – 1962. At least 3 issues published.

Pictorials, nonfiction, fiction.

Nudes de Paree

Seventy Seventy-One Publications, Hollywood CA.

Early 1960's? How many issues published?

Pictorials.

Nugget

Nugget Inc., New York NY.

November 1955 – 2006. 300+ issues.

Fiction, pictorials.

This title published some really high-quality authors during its run. It eventually devolved into a hardcore pornography rag, of course.

Note: The first couple of years' worth of issues featured interesting background textures on the covers – i.e., fur, leather, etc.

Night Out

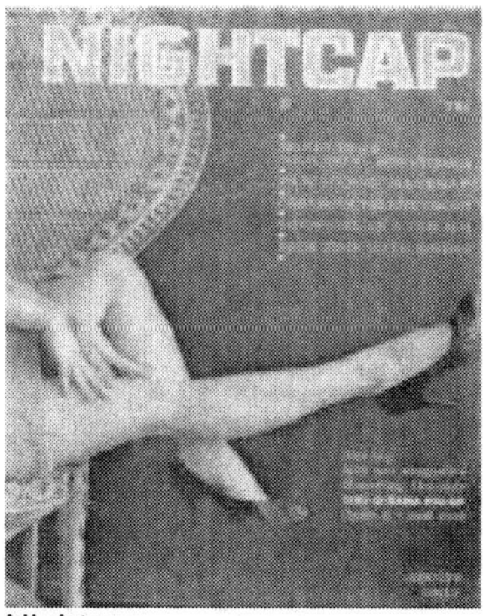

Nightcap

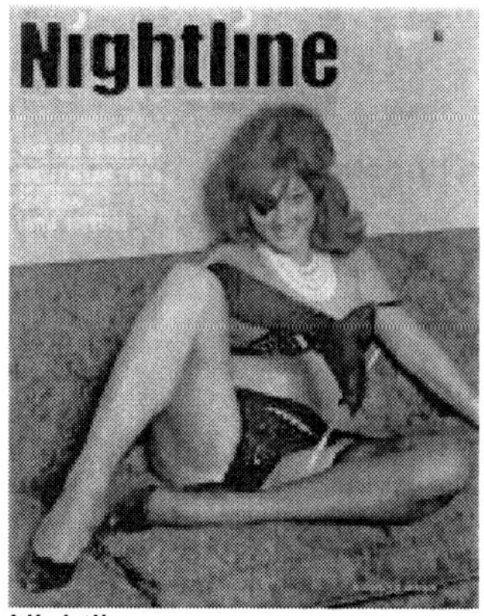

Nightline

Nite Out

Nite'ee

Nocturne

Nugget

Nugget

Nugget

Nylon Double Take
Press Arts Inc., Canoga Park CA.
1960's. At least 10 issues published.
Pictorials.

Nylon Jungle
American Art Agency / Jaybird Enterprises, North Hollywood CA (Parliament).
1962 – 1970's. 30+ issues.
Pictorials.

Nylon Legs
1963. More than 1 issue published?
Pictorials, cartoons.

Nylon Mesh
'The latest of adults entertainment.'
1960's. One-shot?
Pictorials.

Nylon Mood
Sampson Publishing and Distribution Co., New York NY.
1963 – ? At least 3 issues published.
Pictorials.

Nylon Party
American Art Agency, North Hollywood CA (Parliament).
1960's – early 1970's. ~35 issues.
Pictorials.

Nymph
WAKE Publishing Co., San Francisco CA.
1957 – 1958? How many issues were published?
Pictorials, cartoons.

Nymph
Sari Publishing Co., North Hollywood CA.
1961 – 1966? ~12 issues.
Pictorials.

Nymph
Seven Seventy Publishers, North Hollywood CA.
1965. One-shot?
Pictorials.

Nylon Double Take

Nylon Jungle

Nylon Legs

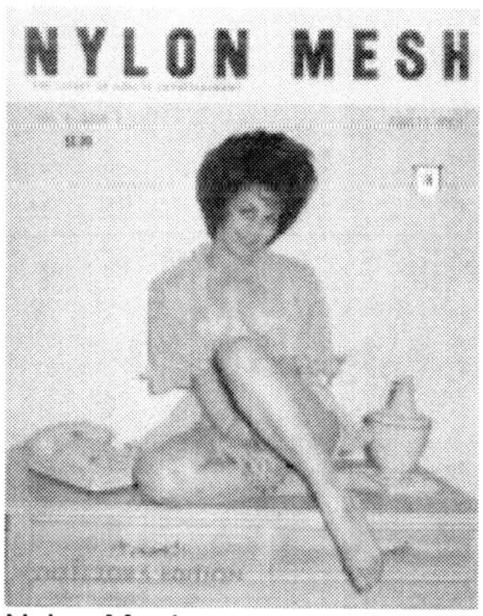

Nylon Mesh

Nylon Mood

Nylon Party

Nymph (Wake)

Nymph (Sari)

Nymph (770)

Off Campus
Campus Enterprises.
December 1962. More than 1 issue exists?
This was obviously an attempt at a men's magazine aimed at college-aged guys.

Ogle
True Problems Publications Inc., New York NY.
March 1956 – 1960? How many issues?
Pictorials, nonfiction, cartoons.
This title was edited by Myron Fass.

OK For Men
Banner Magazines Inc.
December 1958 – August 1959.
Adventure fiction.

Ooh La La!
Health Knowledge Inc., New York NY.
1960's. ~10 issues published.
Pictorials.

Orbit
Selbee Associates Inc., New York NY.
Black and white interiors.
Early 1960's. How many issues?
Pictorials.
It appears there are two issues numbered v.1 #1.
Also shown as *Girls in Orbit* on some covers.

Outdoor Adventures
Outdoor Adventures Publications (Weider).
August 1955 – April 1959. 23 issues.
Adventure fiction.
As one might expect, this title's fiction had a decidedly outdoors/hunting theme.

Pace
Ardee Publications, New York NY.
January 1950 – March 1951. 7 issues.
Nonfiction, pictorials.

Pad
Century Distributors Inc., Van Nuys CA.
June 1968 – ? How many issues of this were published?
Pictorials, nonfiction, fiction, cartoons.

Off Campus

Ogle

OK For Men

OK For Men

Ooh La La

Orbit

Outdoor Adventures

Outdoor Adventures

Pad

Pagan
American Art Agency Inc., Hollywood CA (Parliament).
1962 – 1971? ~30 issues.
Pictorials.

Pale Hose
Early 1960's. How many issues were published?
Pictorials.

Pamper
Black and white interiors with incidental color, and color centerfolds.
1960's. At least 3 issues published?

Paree
Sampson Publishing and Distribution Co., New York NY.
1961. More than 1 issue published?
Pictorials.

Paris Life
Charlton Publications, Derby CT.
1951 – 1958. 35 issues.
Pictorials, nonfiction.

Paris Taboo
Selbee Associates Inc., New York NY.
1959 – 1964. 4 issues.
Pictorials, fiction, nonfiction, cartoons.

Parisian Playgirl
Seventy Seventy-One Publications, Hollywood CA.
1963 – 1964? At least 2 issues produced.
Pictorials, nonfiction, fiction.

Parisien Party
PEC Publications.
1965 – 1966. At least 5 issues.
Pictorials, nonfiction, fiction.

Party Doll
1965 – ? More than 1 issue produced?
Pictorials, fiction.

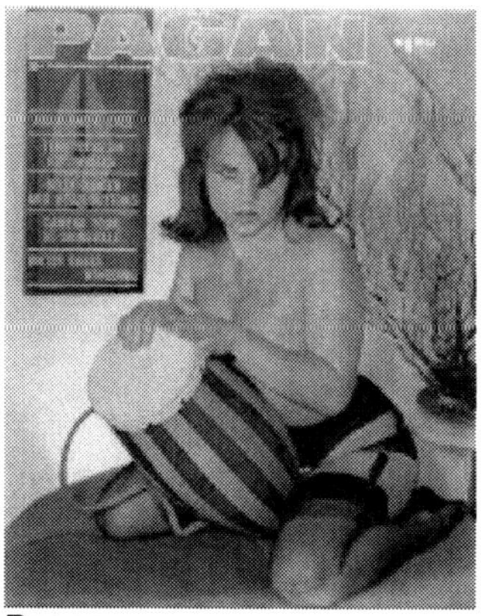

Pagan

Pagan

Pale Hose

Paree

Paris Life

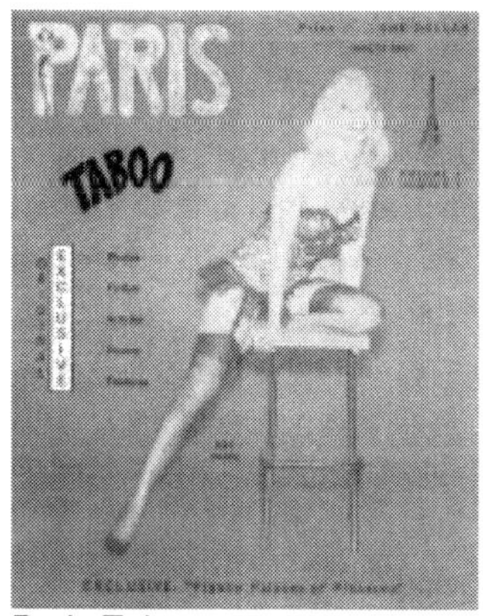

Paris Taboo

Parisian Playgirl

Parisien Party

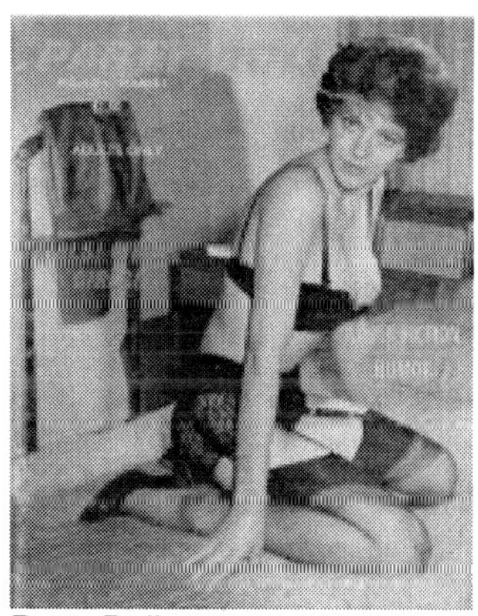
Party Doll

Party Play Gals

Bruce-Royal Publishing, Derby CT.

Summer 1963. One-shot?

Nonfiction, pictorials, cartoons.

Party Time

American Art Agency Inc., Hollywood CA (Parliament).

Late 1960's. 4 issues?

Pictorials.

Not to be confused with a more hardcore Regency title from the early 1970's.

Passion

Patra Publications / Caesar Publishers Inc., New York NY.

Black and white interiors, with color centerfolds.

1962 – ? ~10 issues published?

Pictorials, nonfiction.

Peek-A-Boo

Health Knowledge Inc., New York NY.

Black and white interiors, with color centerfolds.

1966 – ? At least 10 issues produced.

Pictorials.

Issues appeared infrequently.

Peek-A-Book

1956. One-shot?

Pictorials.

This was apparently a gimmick mag in that the (semi) nude photos were partially obscured but could be seen with a simple trick.

Peep Show

Capitol Stories Inc. / N.E.W.S. Publishing Corp., Derby CT (Charlton).

Black and white interiors. Measures 9.5 by 12.5 inches.

Winter 1950 – May 1958. 34 issues.

Pictorials.

People Today

Hillman Periodicals Inc., New York NY.

June 1950 – late 1960's? 200+ issues.

Black and white interiors. Measured 4 by 6 inches.

Nonfiction, pictorials.

This title's light mix of popular articles and gorgeous women allowed it to survive for decades.

Note that, although the title ran well into the 1960's, the 1950's issues are by far more commonly found.

Party Play Gals

Party Time

Passion

Passion

Peek-A-Boo

Peek-A-Book

Peep Show

Peep Show

People Today

Pepper
Selbee Associates Inc., New York NY.
Black and white interiors.
1961 – 1962; Winter 1965? – Fall 1967. 8 issues total?
Pictorials, nonfiction.

Pepper Pot
Anchor Publications, Gardena CA.
1965. More than 1 issue produced?

Peril
Jeflin Publications; Periodical Packagers.
October 1956 – March 1963. 36 issues?
Fiction, nonfiction, pictorials.
This title became *Man's Peril* with v.6 #7.

Pet
Black and white interior, with color centerfold.
1963. More than 1 issue produced?
Pictorials.

Photo
Magazine Management, New York NY (Atlas).
June 1952 – May 1956. 39 issues.
Nonfiction, pictorials.

Photo
Official Magazine Corp., New York NY.
July 1964 – 1970's. ~100 issues.
Nonfiction, pictorials.

Photo Life
Lux Publications Inc., New York NY.
Black and white interior.
October 1958 – 1962? Over 20 issues published.
Nonfiction, pictorials.

Photographers Masterpieces
Skye Publishing Co., New York NY.
1957. One-shot.
Pictorials.
This magazine focused upon the efforts of photographer Philip O. Stearns.

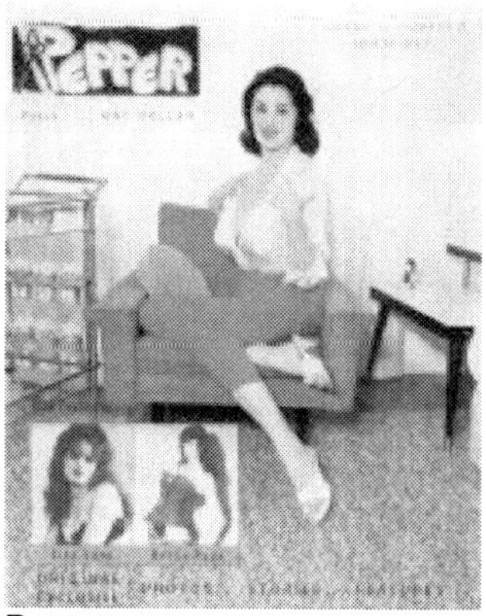

Pepper

Pepper Pot

Peril

Peril

Pet

Photo (1952)

Photo (1964)

Photo Life

Photog's Masterpieces

Photographers Oddball

Skye Publishing Co., New York NY.

1957. Only 1 issue?

Pictorials, nonfiction.

This little oddity had one feature that allowed the reader to cut out and assemble a small photo of Bettie Page.

Photographer's Showplace

Creative Publications, New York NY.

July 1956 – November 1957. 3 or 4 issues?

Pictorials, nonfiction, cartoons.

This title was well-designed and interesting, and featured some of the most beautiful women of the time within its pages. It's a shame it couldn't have lasted longer.

Photographic Artist

House of Price Publications, Northridge CA.

Late 1960's – early 1970's. At least 6 issues published.

Pictorials.

This and the next entry are two entirely separate publications, but because they both overlapped chronologically, and the cover logos tended to change over several issues, it's easy to confuse issues of the one with those of the other.

Photographic Artist

'The erotic art of the lens.'

Ed Lea, Sherman Oaks CA.

Late 1960's. At least 12 issues published?

Pictorials.

Photography For Men

Sterling Group, New York NY.

1957 – 1958. 3 issues.

Pictorials.

Photoplay Pinups

Bartholomew House Inc., New York NY.

1952 – 1955. 5 issues.

Pictorials.

Pic

Picpix Inc., New York NY; Street & Smith, New York NY; etc.

Black and white interiors. Measures 5 by 7 inches.

1937 – 1970's. 400+ issues?

Starting in the late 1930's as a light, very general all-around interest magazine for men, unfortunately by the early 70's it had gone the way of nearly all such titles and became a pornographic title.

Photographers Showplace

Photographers Showplace

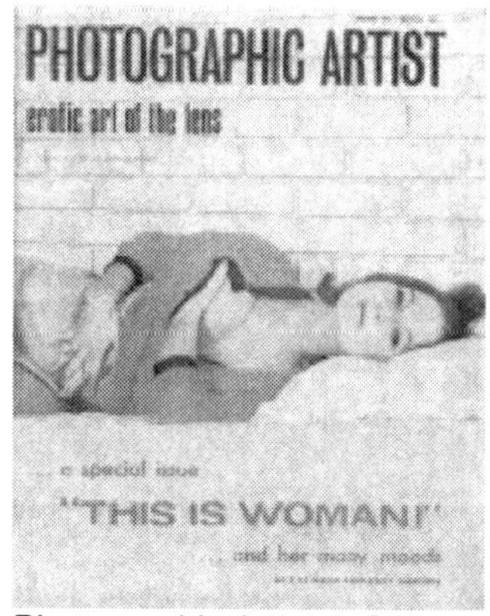

Photographic Artist (HOP)

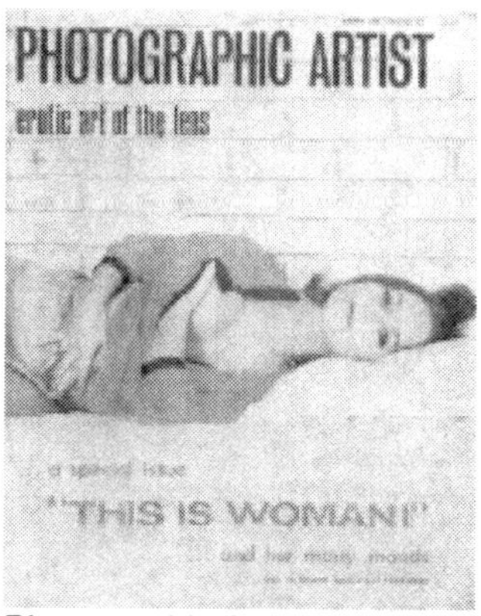

Photographic Artist (Lea)

Photography For Men

Photoplay Pin Ups

Pic

Pic

Pic

A Pictorial Biography of June Wilkinson

Steele Publications.

1961. One-shot.

Pictorials, nonfiction.

As the title suggests, this was an entire magazine devoted to the English glamour model, complete with plenty of photos and biographical articles.

Pictorial Unique

RNS Publications, Los Angeles CA.

1965. Only 2 issues published?

Pictorials, nonfiction, fiction, cartoons.

Picture Digest

Plaza Digest Inc., New York NY.

December 1954 – December 1957. ~20 issues.

Nonfiction, pictorials.

This was a retitling of the previous *Magazine Digest*.

Picture Follies

Manly Publications Inc., New York NY.

November 1951 – June 1953. 9 issue.

Nonfiction, pictorials.

Picture Fun

Volitant Publishing Corp., New York NY.

Black and white interiors. Measures 10 by 13 inches.

December 1951 – January 1953. 5 issues.

Nonfiction, pictorials.

Picture Life

Zenith Publishing Corp., New York NY (Atlas).

Black and white interiors. Measures 4 by 6 inches.

February 1954 – February 1956? 14 issues.

Nonfiction, pictorials.

'Zenith Publishing Corp.' was a subsidiary that Atlas used on some of their titles now and then for some reason, up to about 1964. These even included some of their comic book titles from the Marvel Comics period, such as the original 6-issue run of *The Incredible Hulk*.

Picture Scope

Magtab Publishing, New York NY.

Black and white interiors. Digest –sized.

July 1953 – March 1959; July 1960 – July 1962. 44 issues.

Nonfiction, pictorials.

For its first 4 issues, the title of this mag was simply *Scope*.

Note: This was retitled *Zest* for 6 issues, between May 1959 to April 1960.

...June Wilkinson

Pictorial Unique

Picture Digest

Picture Digest

Picture Follies

Picture Fun

Picture Life

Picture Scope

Picture Scope

Picture Show

Picture Magazines Inc., New York NY.

August 1947 – 1950's. 40+ issues.

Pictorials, nonfiction.

Note: Although the regular magazine seems to have suspended publication in about 1951, there was a Spring 1957 Annual published; how many more issues came out in this later period?

Note also that there was a long-running British publication with this title, which may confuse attempts at cataloguing issues.

Picture Spotlight

Black and white interiors. Measures 5.5 by 7.75 inches.

April – July 1959. 2 issues.

Nonfiction, pictorials.

Picture Week

Pocket Magazines Inc., Atlanta GA.

Black and white interiors. Measures 4 by 6 inches.

February 26, 1955 – July 3, 1958. 60+ issues.

Nonfiction, pictorials.

Pink Lady

Mid-1960's. How many issues were published?

Pin-Up Fun

Health Knowledge Inc., New York NY.

1967 – 1971. 15 issues?

Pictorials.

Pin-Up Photography

Charlton Publications, Derby CT.

Mid-1950's. How many issues?

Nonfiction, pictorials.

The Spring 1956 issue features Bettie Page on the cover.

Pip

Pip Publishing Co., North Hollywood CA.

1960's. More than 1 issue published?

Pictorials.

Pique

1963. More than 1 issue published?

Pictorials.

Picture Show

Picture Show

Picture Spotlight

Picture Week

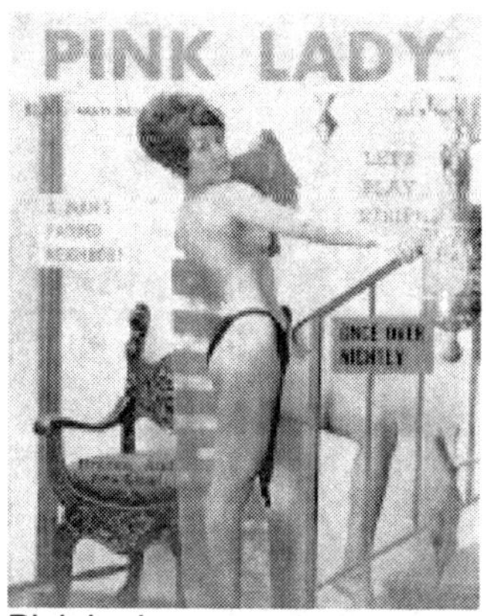

Pink Lady

Pin-Up Photography

Pip

Pique

Pix (1949)

Pix

'A picture look at life.'

Picturight Inc., New York NY.

Black and white interiors. Measures 10 by 13 inches.

August 1949 –1958? ~40 issues.

Nonfiction, pictorials.

Note: the last several issues from about 1954 on were called *Pix Annual* and appeared quarterly.

Pix

Knight Publishing Corp., Los Angeles CA.

Black and white and monochromatic interiors.

1963 – 1977. ~75 issues.

Pictorials, fiction, nonfiction.

Thick covers on this magazine which, as the title implies, is heavy with nude photos.

Pixie

Comet Publications, Los Angeles CA; Classic Publications, Los Angeles CA.

1965 – 1973. How many issues?

Pictorials, nonfiction, fiction.

Were there two magazines with this title, or did Classic Publications take over the title from Comet? In any case, the earlier issues of this were more general text-and-photo men's magazines, while the 70's issues were predictably more pornographic.

Plaisir

1960's. More than 1 issue published?

Play

Screen Teen Co., Purchase NY.

February 1954. Only 1 issue published?

Nonfiction, pictorials.

Play

'Showgirls – models – pinups.'

Lucky Magazines Inc., New York NY.

1959 – 1961? ~8 issues published?

Pictorials.

Play-Dates

Bruce-Royal Publishing, Derby CT.

Mid-1960's. More than 4 issues published?

Pictorials, nonfiction, cartoons.

Pix (1949)

Pix (1963)

Pix (1963)

Pixie

Plaisir

Play (Screen Teen Co.)

Play (Lucky)

Play (Lucky)

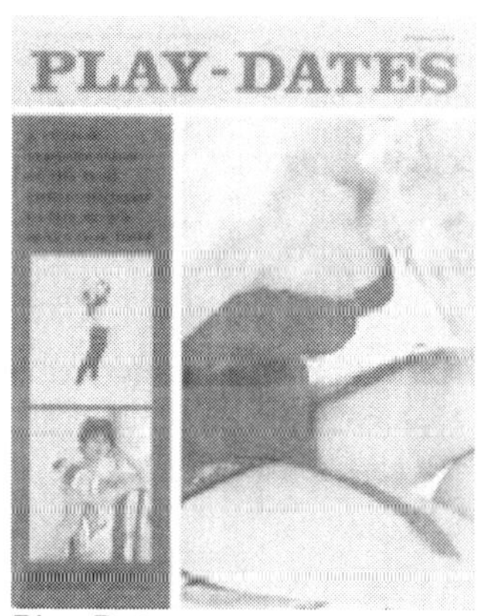

Play-Dates

Play-Things

Bruce-Royal Publishing, Derby CT.

Fall 1964. One-shot?

Pictorials, nonfiction, fiction, cartoons.

Playboy

HMH Publishing Co., Chicago IL.

December 1953 – Present. 600+ issues, plus various specials.

Pictorials, fiction, nonfiction.

Although not quite the first modern men's magazine, it was *Playboy* that captured the larger public's imagination and which rose to a level of success that no one else has been able to approach. Much of this was due to publisher Hugh Hefner's attention to quality, as well as his refusal to accept anything less than the highest quality content or advertising.

Playgirl

Playgirl Publishing Co., San Francisco CA.

Mid-1950's. At least 4 issues published.

Nonfiction, pictorials.

Not related with the female version of *Playboy*, of course.

Playtime

'Fun for fellows and femmes.'

New Publishing Co., Los Angeles CA.

Black and white interiors.

1958. Only 1 issue published?

Pictorials, nonfiction, fiction, cartoons.

Playtime

'The new fun magazine for males!'

Art Enterprises Inc., Los Angeles CA.

Black and white interiors with color centerfolds.

1960's. More than 2 issues published?

Pictorials, nonfiction.

Please

New Link Publications, Los Angeles CA.

1960's. At least 12 issues published?

Pictorials, nonfiction.

Pleasure

Art Enterprises Inc., Los Angeles CA.

1960. 4 issues.

Nonfiction, pictorials.

Play-Things

Playboy

Playboy

Playgirl

Playtime (New Pub.)

Playtime (Art Enterprises)

Playtime (Art Enterprises)

Please

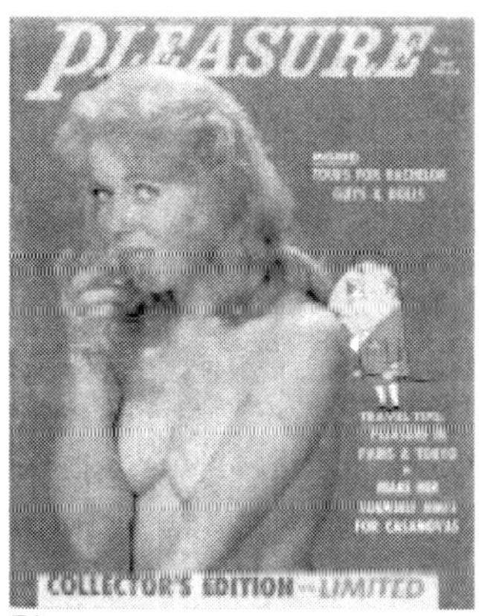

Pleasure

Pleasure Cruise

1962. Just 1 issue published?

Pictorials.

Plowboy

Bannister Publishing Co.

Spring 1957. One-shot.

Humor, pictorials, nonfiction, fiction.

This is obviously a parody of the popular *Playboy*. Every item is a spoof of Hefner's usual fare; each fiction piece is written by a writer with the first name of Max, for example (i.e., Max Faulkner, Max Hemingway, etc.). It does feature genuine nudes, though, so it certainly qualifies for inclusion in this volume.

Plush

'Living For Men.'

Emengee Publications, Inc., New York NY.

Black and white interior.

December 1958 – 1960. 10 regular issues plus 1 Annual.

Fiction, nonfiction, pictorials, cartoons.

Pocket Pinups

Authentic Publications

Black and white interiors. Measures 4 by 6 inches.

1955. Only 2 issues?

Pictorials.

Point (Of View)

See *Male Point of View*.

Poorboy

Tempest Publications, New York NY.

May – November 1968? At least 3 issues.

Pictorials, nonfiction.

Although this may at first appear to be a fake *Playboy* parody, this was actually a late-60's attempt to make a nudie pictorial mag with the sensibilities of the then-popular hippie movement.

Popular Cartoons

Visual Varieties Inc., New York NY (Atlas).

Black and white interiors. Measures 5.5 by 7.5 inches.

1967 – 1981. ~60 issues.

Cartoons, pictorials.

This was another subsidiary of the same publisher as Marvel Comics.

Pleasure Cruise

Plowboy

Plush

Plush

Pocket Pinups

Pocket Pinups

Poorboy

Popular Cartoons

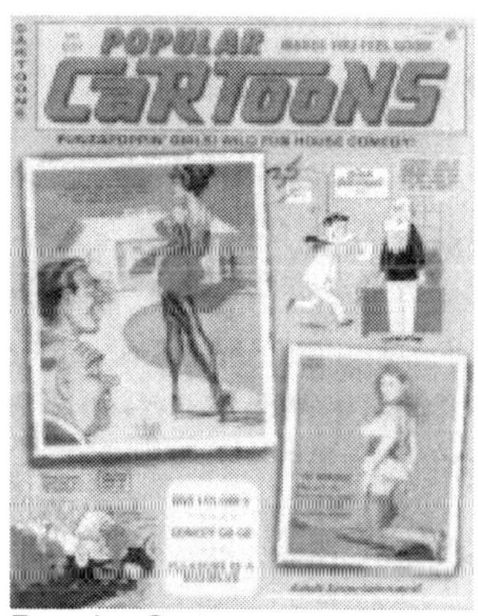

Popular Cartoons

Popular Jokes
Visual Varieties Inc., New York NY (Atlas).
Black and white interiors. Measures 5.5 by 7.5 inches.
August 1961 – August 1981. ~80 issues.
Cartoons, pictorials.

Pose
Cape Magazine Management Corp., New York NY.
1954 – October 1960? 40+ issues.
Pictorials.
Was this previously *Pulse*?

Potpourri
1960's. More than 1 issue?

Preview
Patra Publications, New York NY.
1960's. How many issues published?

Prevue
Madison Publishing Co.
Black and white interiors. Measures 4 by 6 inches.
1950's. How many issues published?
Nonfiction, pictorials.

Primadonna
1960's. How many issues were published?

Prince
Rilgac Publishing Co., Hollywood CA.
1960 – 1962. 5 issues.
Pictorials.

Private Line
Health Knowledge Inc., New York NY.
Black and white interiors, with color centerfolds.
1960's. At least 10 issues.
Pictorials, nonfiction, fiction.

Prize Sea Stories
Macfadden Publications.
Spring 1964. One-shot?
Adventure fiction.
Mostly reprints from *Saga* magazine, this seems to have been a one-off.

Popular Jokes

Pose

Pose

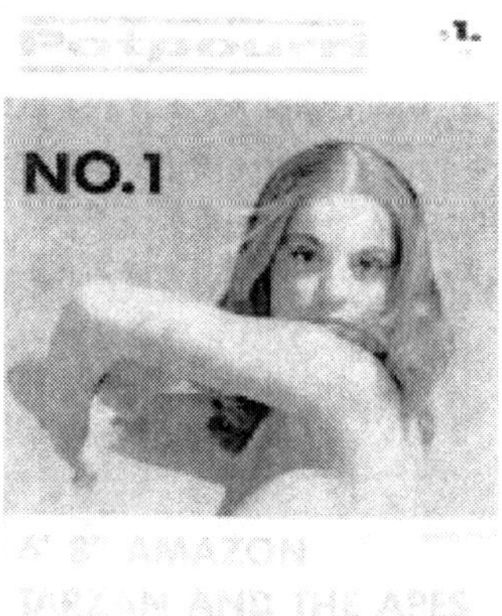

Potpourri

Prevue

Primadonna

Prince

Private Line

Private Line

Professional Photography

1957. One-shot?

Pictorials, nonfiction.

Pulse

Dodshaw Publishing Corp., New York NY.

Pocket-sized.

October 1954 – September 1955.

Nonfiction, pictorials.

Purr-r

Caesar Publishers Inc., New York NY.

1960's. ~10 issues?

Pictorials.

Pussycat

Chelsea Publishing Co., Hollywood CA (Parliament).

1966 – 1973? At least 25 issues, plus at least 1 Annual.

Pictorials.

This magazine eventually concentrated only on African-American models.

Note: This publication is not related to the 1966 Pussycat Calendar from World Wide News Corp., nor the comic-strip collection *The Adventures of Pussycat* released by Magazine Management (aka Atlas, aka Marvel Comics).

Quick

Digest-sized.

1954 – 1961. 30+ issues.

Nonfiction, pictorials.

Quick

'The original newspaper magazine.'

Tempest Publications, New York NY.

October 1964 – June 1965. 5 issues.

Nonfiction, pictorials.

Quickie

American Art Agency, Hollywood CA (Parliament).

Measures 5.5 by 8.5 inches.

1962 – 1966? ~10 issues.

Pictorials, nonfiction.

Rage

'The magazine for men.'

Natlus Inc.

September 1960 – July 1964. 18 issues.

Professional Photography

Pulse

Purr-r

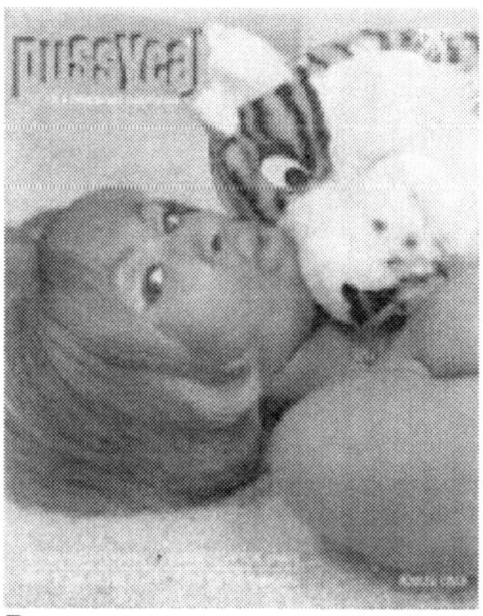
Pussycat

Pussycat

Quick (digest)

Quick (Tempest)

Quickie

Rage (Natlus)

Fiction, nonfiction, pictorials.

This was simply *Rage* up until the May 1963 issue, when it became *Rage For Men*. But it was apparently not related to the earlier magazine that started in 1956 (see next entry).

Rage For Men

Arnold Magazines Inc., Stamford CT.

December 1956 – February 1958. 8 issues.

Adventure fiction, pictorials.

Rake

'The magazine for males only.'

Model Books Inc.

January – July 1962. 3 issues.

Fiction, nonfiction, pictorials.

Rapture

Beacon Publications, Studio City CA.

Black and white interiors, with color centerfolds.

1959 – 1961? At least 4 issues published.

Nonfiction, fiction, pictorials.

Rapture

American Art Agency, Hollywood CA (Parliament).

1963 – 1973? 42 issues?

Pictorials.

Rare & Rugged

Comet Publications, Los Angeles CA.

1964. More than 2 issues published?

Rascal

Camerarts Publishing Co., Chicago IL.

1957 – 1977? 100+ issues.

Pictorials, nonfiction.

Did this magazine take a hiatus somewhere between 1957 and 1963? Note that the 1957 issues (more than 2?) were digests, measuring 5.25 by 8.25 inches.

Rave

'The magazine of intimate expose.'

Rave Publishing Corp., New York NY.

Digest-sized.

April 1953 – 1958. 23 issues?

Nonfiction, pictorials.

This was primarily a scandal/celebrity dirt title in many ways, but always with a masculine slant, and enough glamour pictorials to justify its inclusion in this book.

Rage For Men

Rage For Men

Rake

Rapture (Beacon)

Rapture (Parliament)

Rapture (Parliament)

Rascal

Rascal

Rave

Raven

Sampson Publishing and Distribution Co., New York NY.

Early 1960's. One-shot?

Pictorials.

Raw!

Press Arts Inc., Canoga Park CA.

Black and white interiors, with color covers.

1960's. More than 15 issues?

Pictorials, nonfiction.

Apparently the tenth issue bore the title *Raw! Reader* on the cover.

Real

Literary Enterprises Inc.; Excellent Publications; PAR Publications; Arizill Realty and Publishing. (Were these separate companies, subsidiaries of a larger company, or what?)

October 1952 – December 1967. 100+, including at least 1 Annual.

Nonfiction, fiction.

True to its title, this magazine primarily dealt with nonfiction articles and stories.

Real Action

Normandy Associates, New York NY (Stanley).

June 1963 – June 1964. 7 issues.

Fiction, nonfiction, pictorials.

Real Action For Men

Four Star Publications, New York NY.

April 1957 – January 1958. 5 issues.

Fiction, nonfiction.

Real Adventure

Hillman Periodicals Inc., New York NY.

March 1955 – November 1958; November 1960 – May-June 1961; September – November 1963.

27 issues?

Adventure fiction, non-fiction.

It's not clear why this title had such a stuttering publishing schedule. Note that the later title by Jalart House (see next entry) seems to have been a completely different publication.

Real Adventures

Jalart House, New York NY.

April 1969 – July 1971? 10 issues plus 3 Annuals?

Pictorials, nonfiction, fiction.

This seems to be a completely different title from the previous *Real Adventure* from Hillman. This one was certainly more girlie-oriented.

Note: The last two issues were titled *Real Adventure* on the cover.

Raw

Raw

Real

Real

Real Action

Real Action For Men

Real Adventure

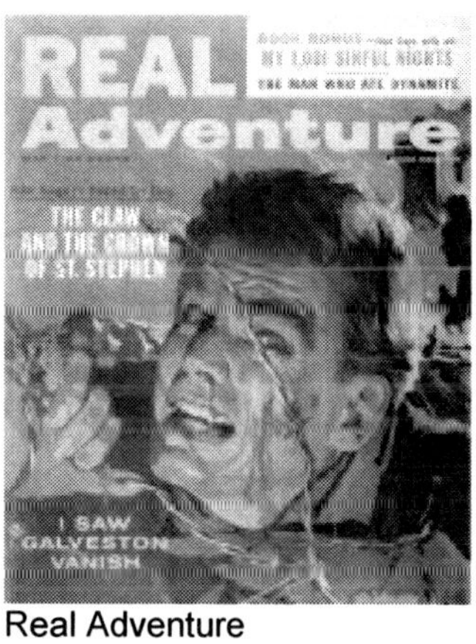

Real Adventure

Real Adventures

Real Combat Stories

Reese Publishing Co., New York NY

October 1963 – April 1972. 34 issues.

Adventure fiction, nonfiction, pictorials.

As the title implies, the emphasis is on wartime action.

Real Life Adventures

Vista Publications, New York NY (Atlas).

October 1957 – February 1958? 3+ issues?

Adventure fiction.

Probably a retitling of a previous magazine, taking over the numbering.

Real Men

Stanley Publications, New York NY.

March 1956 – February 1975. 100+ issues.

Adventure fiction, nonfiction, pictorials.

This title started as a regular men's adventure fiction magazine, then started transitioning in the mid-60's with more women portrayed on the covers, and the artwork gradually de-emphasized. By the end it was a nudie girlie mag with sex-oriented nonfiction.

Real War

Stanley Publications, New York NY.

October 1957 – November 1958. 9 issues.

Adventure fiction, nonfiction.

Combat-oriented fiction, as the title implies.

The Rebel Breed

Press Arts Inc., Canoga Park CA.

Late 1960's. At least 2 issues.

Pictorials, nonfiction.

Red Garter

International Publications Inc., Hollywood CA.

1962 – 1963. 5 issues.

Pictorials, nonfiction, fiction.

Relax

Finesse Publications Inc., New York NY.

May – September 1957. 3 issues.

Fiction, nonfiction, pictorials.

Rendezvous (With Pleasure)

Art Enterprises Inc., Los Angeles CA.

Early 1960's. ~10 issues published.

Pictorials, nonfiction.

Real Combat Stories

Real Life Adventures

Real Men

Real Men

Real War

Rebel Breed

Red Garter

Relax

Rendezvous With Pleasure

Restless

1960's. How many issues were published?

Retreat

Comet Publications, Los Angeles CA.

Black and white interiors, with color centerfolds.

1963 – 1965? 6+ issues published.

Pictorials, nonfiction.

Note: There is also a 'Retreat 1968 Yearbook.' Is that part of this series, or from another publication altogether?

Revels

Art Enterprises Inc., Los Angeles CA.

1958 – 1962. 6 issues.

Pictorials, nonfiction.

Rex

Delta Publishing Corp., New York NY.

Black and white and color interior.

October – December 1957. 3 issues.

Fiction, nonfiction, pictorials, cartoons.

This title had a very brief run despite carrying the work of some top-name writers; but it apparently didn't quite have enough nude photography to appeal to the potential readership.

Rhapsody

American Art Agency, Hollywood CA (Parliament).

Early 1960's. 4 issues?

Pictorials, nonfiction.

Rif Raf

1963. More than 1 issue published?

Pictorials.

Risk For Men

Magnum Publications Inc., New York NY.

Black and white interiors. Measures 4 by 6 inches.

March – July 1957. 4 issues.

Nonfiction, pictorials.

Rizgay

Rilgac Publishing Co., Hollywood CA.

1962. More than 1 issue published?

Pictorials.

Restless

Retreat

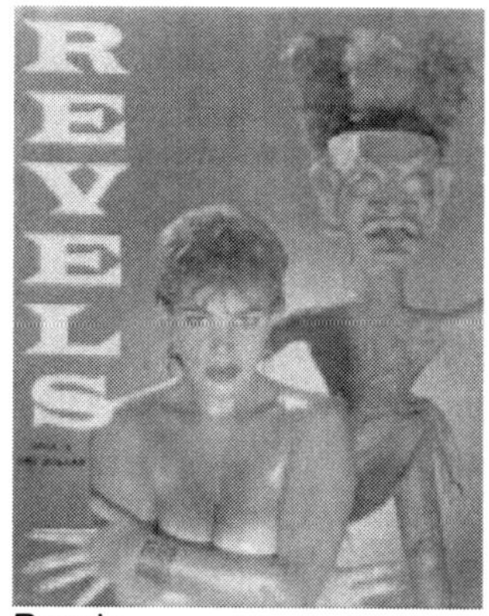

Revels

Revels

Rex

Rhapsody

Rif Raf

Rizgay

Rogue

Rogue

Greenleaf Publishing Co., Evanston IL; Douglas Publishing, Los Angeles CA.

December 1955 – 1977? 150+ issues, including various Annuals.

Pictorials, fiction, nonfiction, cartoons.

This magazine was pretty high-quality for a long time, and even sported a column by Lenny Bruce for a little over a year (about 1961). It devolved into pure pornography by the mid-70's, though.

Romp

Humorama Inc., New York NY (Atlas).

Black and white interiors. Measures 5.5 by 7.5 inches.

1960 – 1971? 65+ issues.

Cartoons, pictorials.

Romp

Triumph News Co. Inc., Van Nuys CA.

Black and white interior?

April 1968 – July 1969? 8 issues?

Fiction, nonfiction, pictorials.

Did this title change to *Romp Set* at one point?

Romper

Late 1960's. Only 1 issue?

Round the World

Sampson Publishing and Distribution Co., New York NY.

1960's. Only 1 issue?

Rugged

Stanley Publications Inc., New York NY.

February – August 1957? 4 issues?

Fiction, nonfiction, pictorials.

Though the covers suggested plenty of female skin, the interiors were mostly articles and fiction stories like most magzines of the time. The second issue did have Bettie Page on the cover and in a few smaller photos inside, though.

Rugged Men

Stanley Publications Inc., New York NY.

April 1956 – March 1959; October 1960 – June 1961. 18 issues.

Adventure fiction, nonfiction.

This title was called *Spur* on the cover for 4 issues in 1959, for some reason.

Rogue

Rogue

Romp (Humorama)

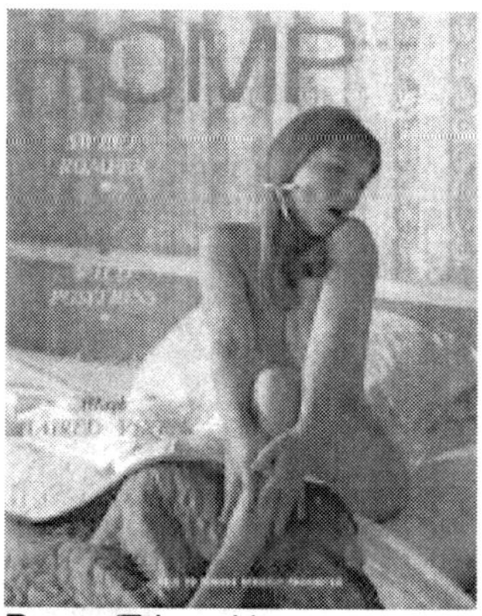

Romp (Triumph)

Romper

Round the World

Rugged

Rugged Men

Rugged Men

Sable
Tri-S Publications, Hollywood CA.
Black and white interiors, with color centerfolds.
1959 – 1963? How many issues were published?
Pictorials, nonficiton.

Safari
Safari Publications (Weider?).
July? 1955 – February 1958. ~20 issues.
Adventure fiction.
This title took over the numbering of *Animal Life*.
Note: Very collectable, this magazine had some gorgeous covers during its short run.

Saga
Macfadden Publications; Gambi Publications.
September 1950 – 1981? 100+ issues, plus several Annuals.
Nonfiction, fiction.
This magazine, which lasted through three decades, maintained an emphasis throughout its run on nonfiction articles. By the end it had become a bit more celebrity-oriented.

Sahara
1960's. How many issues were published?
Pictorials, nonfiction.

Salome
1961. More than 1 issue produced?
Pictorials.

Salty
Dominion Publishing Co., North Hollywood CA.
Late 1960's – early 1970's. At least 7 issues published.
Pictorials.

Salvo
January – April 1957. 3 issues.
Adventure fiction.

Sassy
Seven Seventy Publishers, North Hollywood CA.
Early 1960's. At least 5 issues published.
Pictorials.

Sable

Safari

Safari

Saga

Saga

Sahara

Salome

Salty

Salvo

Sassy Lassies

Marst Publishing Co., North Hollywood CA.

1962. More than 1 issue published?

Pictorials, nonfiction.

Satan

Stanley Publications, New York NY.

Black and white and color interiors.

February – September 1957. 6 issues.

Pictorials, fiction, nonfiction, cartoons.

The most demanded issue of this title is certainly the April 1957 number, which features Bettie Page on the cover and inside.

Satana

Selbee Associates Inc., New York NY.

1962 – 1967. At least 15 issues.

Pictorials, nonfiction.

Satan's Scrapbook

American Art Agency, Hollywood CA (Parliament).

1963 – 1967. ~10 issues.

Pictorials.

Satin and Lace

1956. More than 1 issue published?

Pictorials.

Satin and Lace

H-O-C Publishing.

Black and white interiors.

1958. Only 1 issue produced?

Pictorials.

Satin Showplace

American Art Agency, Hollywood CA; Windsor Publishing Co., North Hollywood CA (Parliament).

1963 – 1964; 1970 – 1973?. At least 5-10 issues published.

Pictorials.

This title appeared for a few issues in the early 1960's, then was revived with v.1 #3 in 1970.

Saucy

'The magazine with spice.'

Imperial Publishing Co., Hollywood CA.

Early 1960's? ~10 issues?

Nonfiction, fiction, pictorials.

Sassy Lassies

Satan

Satana

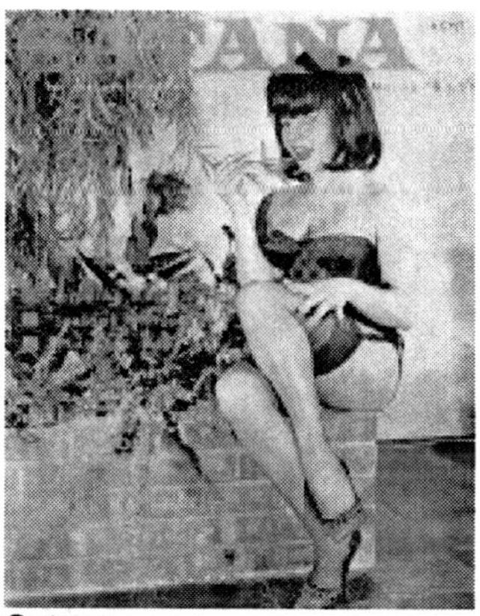

Satana

Satan's Scrapbook

Satin and Lace (1956)

Satin and Lace (1958)

Satin Showplace

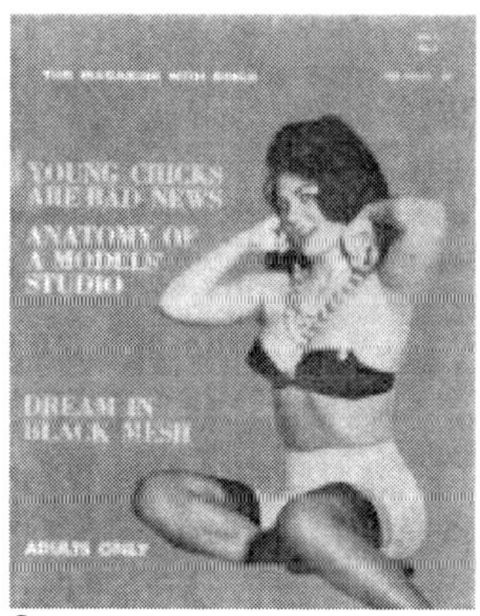

Saucy

Savage Adventure

Matclif Publications, New York NY.

October 1960 – May 1961. 4 issues.

Adventure fiction.

Savage Adventures for Men

Humor Digest, Inc.; Cape Magazine Management Inc., New York NY.

March – September 1959? 3 issues?

Adventure fiction.

This was a retitling of *Brave* near the end of its run.

Scam

Press Arts Inc., Canoga Park CA.

Late 1960's. At least 2 issues published.

Scamp

Splendid Publications, New York NY.

May 1957 – September 1963. 35 issues.

Pictorials, fiction, nonfiction.

This was a pleasant, light mix of girlie photos, fiction, and articles. One of the more commonly-found titles from this era.

Scamp

Knight Publishing Corp., Los Angeles CA.

Black and white interiors, with some color photos.

May 1962. More than 1 issue produced?

Pictorials, nonfiction.

What was Knight Publishing thinking, creating a magazine with this title when the Splendid Pubs. one was so widely known? Was more than one issue created, or just this one, before possibly being threatened with a lawsuit?

Scan

Digest-sized.

1957. At least 2 issues published.

Nonfiction, pictorials.

Scandolls

Scandolls Magazine, New York NY.

1959. More than 1 issue published?

Nonfiction, pictorials, cartoons.

Scantie

Sari Publishing Co., North Hollywood CA.

1962 – ? 5+ issues published?

Pictorials, nonfiction, fiction.

Savage Adventure

Savage Adventure

Savage Adventures For Men

Scamp (Splendid)

Scamp (Splendid)

Scamp (Splendid)

Scamp (Knight)

Scandolls

Scantie (Sari)

Scantie

Seven Seventy One Publications, Hollywood CA.

Black and white interiors, with color centerfold.

1962. One-shot?

Pictorials.

Scanty

1960's. More than 1 issue?

Scarlet

Scarlet Publishing Co.

1957 – 1958. 2 issues.

Nonfiction, pictorials.

Scarlet

Sampson Publishing and Distribution Co., New York NY.

1962 – 1963. 6 issues.

Pictorials, fiction, nonfiction.

Scene

J.B. Publishing, New York NY.

June 1961 – December 1963. 15 issues.

Pictorials, fiction, nonfiction.

This title began as a celebrity/gossip mag in 1954, but within the hobby it is generally agreed that it had fully made the transition to the genre of the modern men's magazine with the June 1961 issue – although an argument could be made for the issues starting in 1958, when the title was actually *Scene For Men*.

Note: The August 1963 issue was titled *American Scene* on the cover.

Scoop

Candid Magazines Inc., New York NY.

October 1953 – July 1954. 8 issues.

Pictorials, nonfiction.

Scope

Magtab Publishing, New York NY.

November 1952 – May 1953. 4 issues.

Nonfiction, pictorials.

This was retitled *Picture Scope* with the 5th issue.

Screen Annual (Pin-Ups)

Skye Publishing Co., New York NY.

1951 – 1962. ~12 issues.

Pictorials, nonfiction.

Scantie (770)

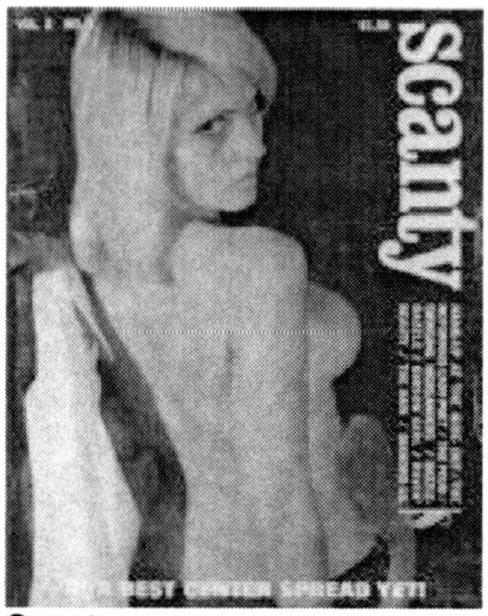

Scanty

Scarlet (Scarlet)

Scarlet (Sampson)

Scene

Scene

Scoop

Scope

Screen Annual Pin-Ups

This was an annual title consisting of pinups of TV and film stars. Only the 1955 issue was called *Screen Annual Pin-Ups*.

Sea Adventures

May 1959. One-shot?

Adventure fiction.

Sea Stories

Future Publications.

Digest size.

November 1953 – March 1954. 2 issues?

Adventure fiction.

See (For Men)

Literary Enterprises; Excellent Publications Inc., New York NY; Par Publications; Arizill Realty Publishing Co., Tucson AZ.

July 1942 – 1968? 100+ issues.

Pictorials, adventure fiction, nonfiction.

For much of its lifetime, this magazine was a good-girl girlie mag. In late 1956 it switched to the men's adventure fiction format, but still retained pictorials. Toward the end (late 60's?) it appeared to move again toward girlie, although – given the changes in the industry at the time – more pornographic than before.

Seize

Press Arts Inc., Canoga Park CA.

1967. At least 4 issues.

Pictorials.

This title was basically a softcore lesbian magazine.

Sensation

Medallion Publishing Corp., New York NY (Atlas).

Black and white interiors. Measures 4 by 6 inches.

January 1954 – February 1955. 11 issues.

Nonfiction, pictorials.

Sensation

Skye Publishing Co., New York NY.

October 1958 – April 1959. 3 issues.

Adventure fiction.

This title changed to *Expose* with its fourth issue, but it must have been a title change from a previous publication, because the first issue is designated v.2, #4.

Sensation

American Art Agency, Hollywood CA.

1963 – 1969. 18-20 issues.

Pictorials.

Sea Adventures

Sea Stories

See For Men

See For Men

Seize

Sensation (Medallion)

Sensation (Skye)

Sensation (Parliament)

Sensation (Parliament)

Sensualist

Billingsley Publications, Hollywood CA.

'A beer drinker's magazine.'

1960. Only 1 issue, apparently.

Nonfiction, pictorials.

Service Snickers

Magnum-Royal Publications, New York NY.

Late 1960's. At least 4 issues published.

Cartoons, pictorials.

This was another cartoon/pinup mag, but this time with a military personnel theme. It was probably sold on military bases in addition to regular distribution.

Seven Seas

Ziff-Davis, New York NY.

1953. One-shot.

Adventure fiction.

This one-off contained new and reprinted fiction material.

Sex & Censorship

Mid-Tower Publishing Corp., San Francisco CA.

1958. 2 issues?

Nonfiction, pictorials.

The second issue contains an article on witch burning by Forrest J. Ackerman.

Sex-Citement

Magnum-Royal Publications, New York NY.

Late 1960's – early 1970's? 1-6 issues?

Cartoons, pictorials.

It's possible that this is the first (perhaps only) issue, as this seems to be the only one that pops up for sale. It also may have been a retitling of *Sex Power!*

Sex Kittens

Sari Publishing Co., North Hollywood CA.

1966. Only 1 issue published?

Pictorials.

Sex Power!

Magnum-Royal Publications, New York NY.

Late 1960's – early 1970's? 2-5 issues?

Cartoons, pictorials.

Was this the same magazine as *Sex-Citement* and *Sexplosion!* with a different cover title?

Sensation (Parliament)

Sensation (Parliament)

Sensation (Parliament)

Sensualist

Seven Seas

Sex & Censorship

Sex-Citement

Sex Kittens

Sex Power

Sexplosion!

Magnum-Royal Publications, New York NY.

Late 1969's. 1-2 issues?

Cartoons, pictorials.

This may have been the exact same magazine as *Sex-Citement* and *Sex Power!* but with a different title.

Sextet

Billingsley Publications, Hollywood CA.

1960. 4 issues.

Pictorials, nonfiction, humor.

Note: The first issue contains a blurb advertising two of the publisher's other titles, *Mr. Cool* and *Sensualist*.

Sextet

Roena Publications, Los Angeles CA.

1960 – 1963? How many issues were published?

Pictorials, fiction, nonfiction.

Sextet

1960's. More than 1 issue?

Pictorials.

A known example has a Golden State News ('GSN') distributor mark on the cover. Was this a continuation of the Roena title under another publisher name, as may have happened with *Mr. Cool*?

She

'The man's picture magazine.'

Cape Magazine Management Corp., New York NY.

Black and white interiors. Digest-sized.

August 1956 – 1960? ~30 issues.

Pictorials.

Sheer

Tri-S Publications, Hollywood CA.

1959 – 1962. 10+ issues.

Fiction, nonfiction, pictorials, cartoons.

Sheer

Spice Publications.

1959 – ? At least 4 issues.

Pictorials.

Sexplosion!

Sextet (Billingsley)

Sextet (Roena)

Sextet (GSN)

She

Sheer (Tri S)

Sheer (Tri S)

Sheer (Spice)

Sheer (Spice)

Sheer Delight
Batters Publications Inc., Hollywood CA.
1958. At least 2 issues published?
Pictorials.
This title might have become *Sheer Hose* later on.

Sheer Hose (1st)
1960's. More than 1 issue published?

Sheer Hose (2nd)
1960's. More than 1 issue published?

Sheer Magic
Modest Publishing Co., Los Angeles CA.
Black and white interiors with color centerfolds.
1963. More than 1 issue?
Pictorials, nonfiction, fiction.

Sheer Magic
Comet Publications, Beverly Hills CA.
1960's. More than 1 issue?

Sheik
ABC Publications, El Monte CA.
Black and white interiors with color centerfold.
1959 – 1960? At least 3 issues plus 1 Annual.
Pictorials.

Shocking Stockings
Sampson Publishing and Distribution Co., New York NY.
Black and white interiors, with color centerfold.
1963. More than 1 issue?
Pictorials.

Short Stories For Men
American Short Stories Corp.
April – August 1959. 3 issues.
Fiction.
This was actually a retitling for the last 3 issues of the very long-running *Short Stories* fiction magazine. For the final couple of years, the title had focused on men's adventure fiction, which was in the ascendant at the time.

Sheer Delight

Sheer Delight

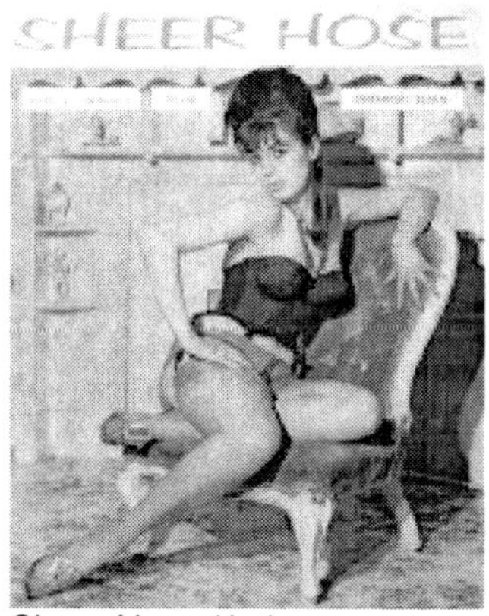

Sheer Hose (1st)

Sheer Hose (2nd)

Sheer Magic (Comet)

Sheik

Sheik

Shocking Stockings

Short Stories For Men

Show
Show Magazine Inc., New York NY.
Black and white interiors. Measures 4 by 6 inches.
September 1952 – November 1957? ~25 issues.
Pictorials, nonfiction.
Not to be confused with the later literature & arts magazine.

Show Off – Girls On Parade
American Art Agency, Hollywood CA (Parliament).
1960's. At least 4 issues published.
Pictorials.

Showboat
American Art Agency, Hollywood CA (Parliament).
1963 – 1971? How many issues?
Pictorials.
This seems to be one of those Parliament titles that takes a hiatus in the mid-1960's only to reappear with higher-numbered issues in 1970-71.

Showcase
American Art Agency, Hollywood CA (Parliament).
1960 – 1965. 15+ issues.
Pictorials.

Showdown For Men
Hanro Corp., New York NY.
November 1957 – November 1958. 7 issues.
Adventure fiction, nonfiction.
This was a retitling of *Men in Combat* with the sixth issue.

Silk Seams
Sampson Publishing and Distribution Co., New York NY.
1963. More than 1 issue published?
Pictorials.

Silky
Synmag Publishing Co., New York NY.
1959 – 1960. 4 issues.
Pictorials.

Silky (2nd)
December 1962. One-shot?
Pictorials.
Was this a continuation of the previous *Silky* title?

Show

Show

Showboat

Showcase

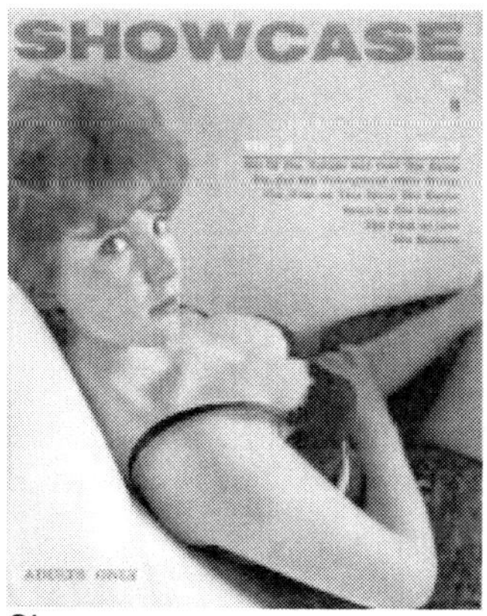

Showcase

Showdown

Silk Seams

Silky (Synmag)

Silky (2nd)

Silky Sirens

N.M. Publications, New York NY.

Black and white interiors.

1962 – 1963. 4 issues.

Pictorials.

Sir!

Volitant Publishing Corp., New York NY.; Histrionic Publishing Co.

June 1942 – June 1984. 400+ issues, not counting several Yearbooks/Annuals.

Pictorials, nonfiction, fiction.

This very long-running title went through several different versions throughout its lifetime, starting as a good-girl pictorial mag, at times becoming a scandal rag and a men's adventure fiction magazine, finally ending up (as so many did) as a pornographic monthly in the mid-80's.

Sir Knight

Sirkay Publishing Co., Los Angeles CA.

1958 – 1962. 33 issues, plus 1 Annual.

Pictorials, nonfiction.

Became just *Knight* with the November 1962 issue.

Note: The omnibus *Knight Treasure Chest* consisted of several issues rebound together.

Siren

Seven Seventy Publishers, North Hollywood CA.

1960's. How many issues published?

Pictorials.

Sizzle

Tri-S Publications, Hollywood CA.

Black and white interiors.

1959 – 1962. 8 issues.

Pictorials.

Issue #8 has the same cover as *Blondes Brunettes Redheads* #3.

Slave

Tuxedo Books Inc. Publishing, New York NY.

1963. More than 1 issue?

Sleek

Black and white interiors, with some color photos.

1960's. 3 issues?

Pictorials.

This was one of those thick compilation magazines that were composed of three or four other magazines rebound under a common cover. So, just seeing the cover for an issue doesn't mean it will match other examples with the same cover.

Was there also another magazine with this title?

Silky Sirens

Sir

Sir

Sir Knight

Sir Knight

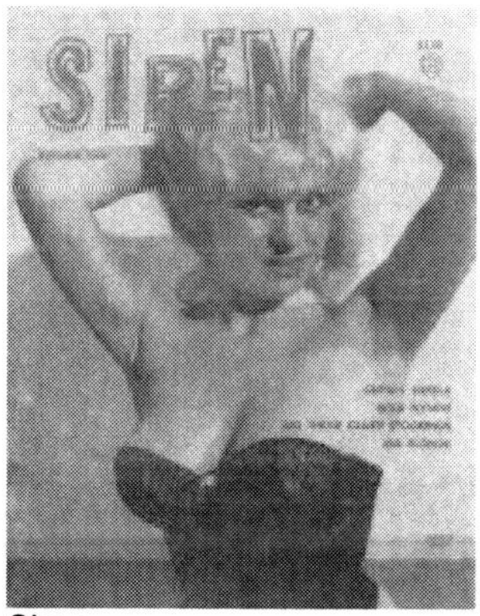

Siren

Sizzle

Slave

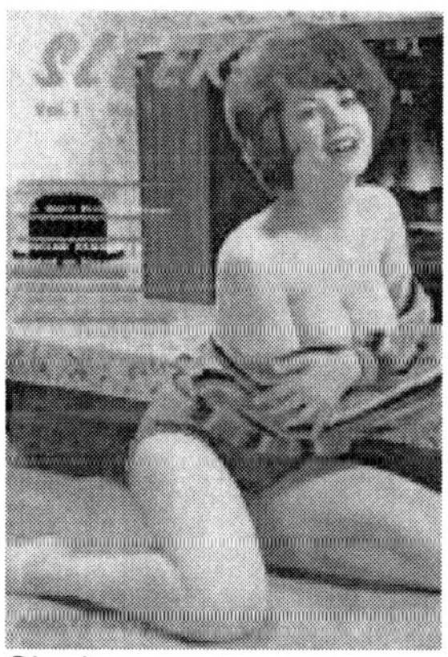
Sleek

Sleek in Hose
Tri-S Publications, Hollywood CA.
1964. 2 issues?
Pictorials, nonfiction.

Slick
'Fun for men.'
Magnum Publications Inc., New York NY.
Black and white interiors. Digest sized.
Late 1950's. How many issues were published?
Pictorials.

Slip & Garter
Comet Publications, Los Angeles CA.
Black and white interiors, with color centerfolds.
1960's. ~20 issues published?
Pictorials, nonfiction.

Smash!
SMASH Publications, Los Angeles CA.
1961 – 1962. 4 issues published.
Pictorials, nonfiction.

Snap
Studio Publications Inc.; Beacon Publications Inc., Studio City CA; American Art Agency, Hollywood CA (Parliament).
1958 – 1970. ~35-40 issues.
Pictorials.

Snappy
Humorama Inc., New York NY (Atlas).
Black and white interiors. Measures 5.5 by 7.5 inches.
1954 – 1962? 50+ issues?
Cartoons, pictorials.

Sneaker World of Elmer Batters
Press Arts Inc., Canoga Park CA.
1969? More than 1 issue?
Pictorials.

Snip
Comet Publications, Los Angeles CA.
1960's. 8-10 issues published?
Pictorials, nonfiction.

Sleek in Hose

Slick

Slip and Garter

Smash

Snap

Snap

Snappy

Sneaker World Of...

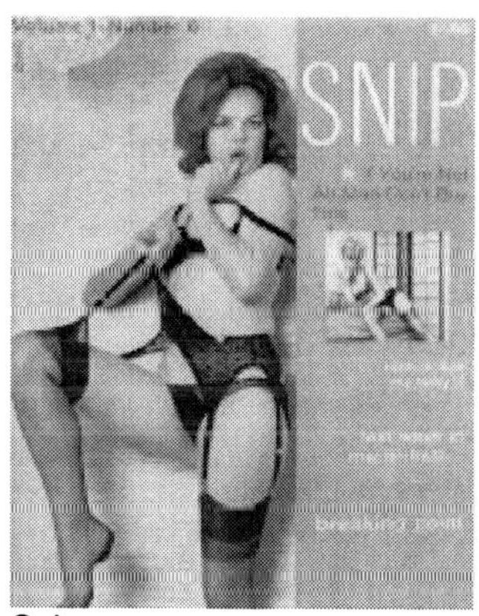

Snip

So Big

World Wide News Co., Cleveland OH.

Black and white interiors, with color centerfolds. Measures 6 by 9 inches.

1966 – 1967? More than 2 issues published?

Pictorials.

South Sea Stories

Counterpoint Inc., New York NY.

July 1960 – November 1964. 24 issues.

Adventure fiction.

Although the title might suggest oceanic adventures, this magazine's stories actually dealt with tales about doings on tropical South Pacific islands.

Spanky

Press Arts Inc., Canoga Park CA.

1966 – 1967. 10 issues published?

Pictorials, nonfiction.

Spark

Delilah Publishing Corp., New York NY.

Early 1960's. More than 1 issue produced?

Pictorials.

Sparkle

American Art Agency, Hollywood CA (Parliament).

1962 – 1964. ~5 issues published.

Pictorials.

Spice

Spice Publications / Tri-S Publications, Hollywood CA.

1959 – 1965. ~10 issues, including at least 1 Annual.

Pictorials.

Spicy Fun

Health Knowledge Inc., New York NY.

1967 – 1970. ~15 issues.

Cartoons, pictorials.

Old-fashioned in its approach and design even with the first issue, it's surprising that this innocent little title lasted as long as it did, given the other fare available (both in humor and erotic photography) at the time.

Splendor

1960's. More than 1 issue published?

So Big

South Sea Stories

Spanky

Spark

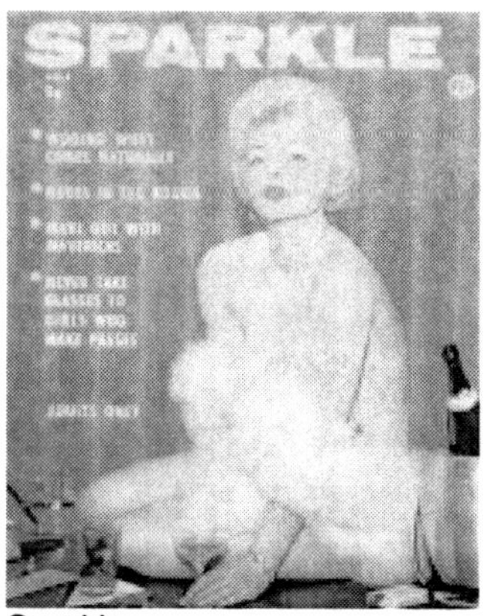

Sparkle

Sparkle

Spice

Spice

Splendor

Sport Adventure

Four Star Publications, New York NY.

June – August 1957. 2 issues.

Adventure fiction.

This title lasted only for 2 issues before being retitled *Ace*.

Sport Life

Select Publications, New York NY (Atlas).

April 1954 – June 1957. 15 issues.

Adventure fiction.

Fiction with an emphasis on big-game hunting and other jungle adventures; each issue's cover featured a wild animal of some sort.

Sport Trails

Atlas Magazines Inc., New York NY.

Summer 1956 – Spring 1957. 4 issues.

Adventure fiction.

Sportsman

Male Publishing, New York NY (Atlas).

April 1953 – April 1968. 70+ issues plus at least 3 large-size special issues.

Adventure fiction, nonfiction, pictorials.

This one started out as a men's adventure mag with an emphasis on jungle tales and wild-animal encounters, before ending up as a girlie-oriented title.

Spree

New Publishing Co., Los Angeles CA.

1958 – 1965? ~45 issues, plus at least 1 Annual.

Fiction, nonfiction, pictorials.

Sprite

Sprite Publishing Co.

1960. At least 3 issues?

Pictorials, nonfiction, fiction.

Spur

Stanley Publications Inc., New York NY.

April – September 1959. 4 issues.

Adventure fiction.

This was a brief retitling of *Rugged Men* for a few months, for whatever reason.

Sport Adventure

Sport Life

Sport Trails

Sportsman

Sportsman

Spree

Spree

Sprite

Spur

Stag

Atlas Magazines Inc., New York NY (under various imprints).

December 1949 – 1978. 300+ issues, plus several larger-size special issues.

Adventure fiction, pictorials, nonfiction.

This long-running monthly title might in many ways be considered Atlas's flagship men's publication. Its history ranged from men's adventure fiction mag to girlie rag.

Star

'People in show business.'

Black and white interiors. Measures 4.25 by 55 inches.

1954. More than 2 issues published?

Nonfiction, pictorials.

Although this was another celebrity-focused pocket magazine, it featured plenty of pinup photos of various models and burlesque dancers.

Star Dust

Delilah Publishing Corp., New York NY.

Black and white interiors, with color centerfolds.

1962. More than 1 issue published?

Pictorials.

Stardust Girls

Tuxedo Books Inc. Publishing, New York NY.

1965. More than 1 issue published?

Pictorials, cartoons.

V. 2 #1 is the one that always pops up; were any others published?

Stare

Humorama Inc., New York NY (Atlas).

Black and white interiors. Measures 5.5 by 7.5 inches.

1951 – 1977? 100+ issues.

Cartoons, pictorials.

Stark

Comet Publications, Los Angeles CA?

1960's. How many issues published?

Stocking Parade

Satellite Publishers, New York NY.

1960. 6 issues.

Stocking Parade

Unique Publications Inc., New York NY.

1965 – 1966. 5 issues.

Pictorials, cartoons, nonfiction.

Stag

Stag

Stag

Star

Stardust Girls

Stare

Stare

Stark

Stocking Parade (Unique)

Stopper

RNS Publications, Los Angeles CA; Comet Publications, Los Angeles CA.

1965 – 1967? ~10 issues?

Pictorials.

Stormy

Dominion Publishing Co., North Hollywood CA.

Late 1960's. At least 5 issues.

Strip

Bonanza Publishing Co., Hollywood CA.

1962. One-shot?

Pictorials, nonfiction, fiction.

Strip-Tease

Health Knowledge Inc., New York NY.

1968. One-shot?

Pictorials.

As the title suggests, this magazine focused upon burlesque strippers, at least the ones that were still going in 1968.

Striparama

Selbee Associates Inc., New York NY.

Black and white interiors, with color centerfolds.

1960 – 1968. ~16 issues.

Pictorials, nonfiction.

Striptease

1960's. At least 4 issues published?

Stud

'A male dominance magazine.'

Press Arts Inc., Canoga Park CA.

1967 – 1968. 3 issues?

Pictorials, nonfiction.

Did this magazine change its title to *Buccaneer*?

Studio A

Sari Publishing Co., North Hollywood CA.

1961. More than 1 issue published?

Pictorials, nonfiction.

Stopper

Stormy

Strip

Strip Tease (one-shot)

Striparama

Striparama

Stud

Stud

Studio A

Sugar

American Art Agency, Hollywood CA (Parliament).

Black and white, with color photos.

1961 – 1968? 6 issues published?

Fiction, nonfiction, pictorials.

Sultry

Press Arts Inc., Canoga Park CA.

1965 – 1969? ~20 issues?

Pictorials, nonfiction.

Swagger

'Every man's magazine.'

Swagger Publications Inc., New York NY.

Black and white interiors.

January – July 1951? 2 issues?

Fiction, nonfiction, pictorials.

Swagger (2nd)

1957 – 1958. 2 issues?

Swagger (3rd)

1965. 4 issues.

Fiction, nonfiction, pictorials.

Note that there was also a magazine called *Swagger* that started in 1969 which doesn't fit into the context of this book, because it was a Marquis Publishing title and all of those were pretty much hardcore.

Swank

Male Publishing Corp. (Atlas), New York NY; Magnum-Royal Publications, New York NY.

Black and white with some color photos, eventually full color.

July 1955 – Present. 600+ issues, plus 1 large-size Special issue.

Nonfiction, pictorials, fiction.

This magazine started out as an Atlas publication but was eventually taken over by Magnum-Royal, and is one of the few old-line men's magazines to survive unto the present day – as a porno mag, of course.

Sway

Sampson Publishing and Distribution Co., New York NY.

Early 1960's. More than 1 issue published?

Swing

Early 1960's? More than 1 issue published?

Sugar

Sultry

Sultry

Swagger (1st)

Swagger (3rd)

Swank

Swank

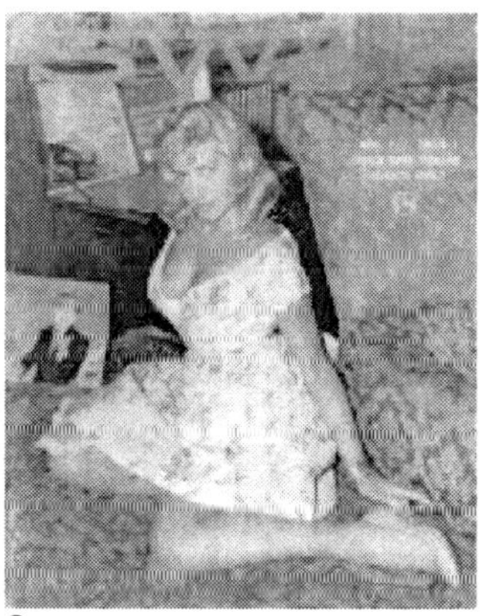

Sway

Swing

Swinger, The
G&S Publications, New York NY.
Black and white interiors, with some color. Measures 8.25 by 10.75 inches.
May 1968 – December 1974. ~40 issues.
Pictorials, nonfiction.

Swingers
Sari Publishing Co., North Hollywood CA.
1964 – 1966? ~10 issues, plus 2 or 3 Annuals.
Pictorials, nonfiction.

Swingle
Magnum-Royal Publications, New York NY.
1968 – 1980? ~50 issues.
Pictorials, nonfiction, cartoons.

Swish
Early 1960's? More than 1 issue published?
Not to be confused with the British nudie mag published between 1978 and 1995.

Tab
'The pocket picture magazine.' Digest-sized.
Carnival Magazine Corp., New York NY.
1951 – 1968? 100+ issues.
Nonfiction, pictorials.

Taboo
Art Enterprises Inc., Los Angeles CA.
October 1949 – December 1950. 10 issues.
Pictorials, nonfiction.
This was a temporary retitling of *Big Time*.

Taboo
American Art Agency Inc., Hollywood CA (Parliament).
Black and white interiors, with color centerfolds.
1960 – 1965. 8 issues.

Tan 'n Terrific
World Wide News Co., Cleveland OH.
Black and white interiors. Measures 6 by 9 inches.
Early 1960's. More than 3 issues produced?
Pictorials.
As the title suggests, this title featured African-American nude models – in fact, according to researcher Jim Linderman, it was the very first magazine to do so.

The Swinger

Swingers

Swingle

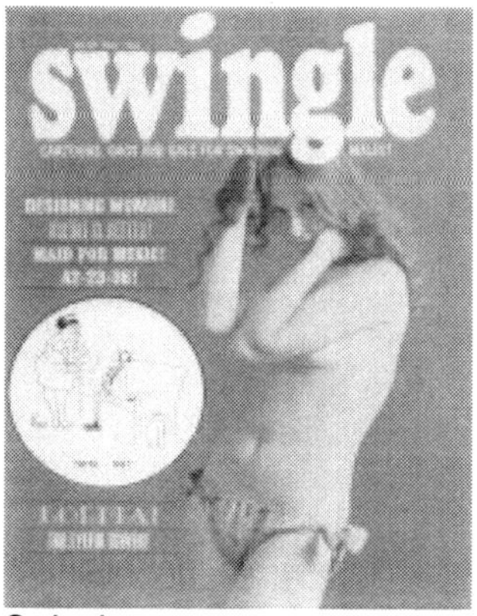

Swingle

Swish

Tab

Tab

Taboo (Art Enterprises)

Tan n' Terrific

Target

VIP Productions.

October 1961 – February 1962. 3 issues.

Adventure fiction.

Tease

Comet Publications, Los Angeles CA; New Link Publications, Hollywood CA.

1960's. 15+ issues?

Pictorials, nonfiction.

Tell

Candid Magazine Corp., New York NY.

Black and white interiors. Measures 6 by 9 inches.

October 1953 – July 1954. 8 issues.

Pictorials, nonfiction.

Tempest

Seven Seventy Publishers, North Hollywood CA.

Early 1960's? At least a handful of issues, including 1 Annual.

Tempo

Pocket Magazines Inc., New York NY.

Black and white interiors. Measures 4 by 6 inches.

1953 – 1963? ~200 issues.

Nonfiction, pictorials.

This was a sort of digest tabloid of the 50's, featuring primarily a lot of celebrity gossip. What qualifies it for this collection was the fact that each issue also showcased one or more beautiful young women. It was weekly for practically its entire run.

Note: For about a year between September 1954 and October 1955, it was properly titled *Tempo & Quick*, although the covers still prominently featured the word *Tempo* for continuity's sake.

Temptee

Selbee Associates Inc., New York NY.

Black and white, and color interiors.

Late 1960's. At least 3 issues?

Pictorials, nonfiction.

That Girl...

Affiliated Magazines Inc.

Black and white interiors. Measures 4 by 6 inches.

Pictorials, nonfiction.

This was a series of 4 small magazines released in 1955, each devoted to a different sex symbol: Marilyn Monroe, Gina Lollobrigida, Anita Ekberg, and Ava Gardner. The title for each was different, for example, *That Girl Marilyn*.

Target

Tease

Tease

Tell

Tempest

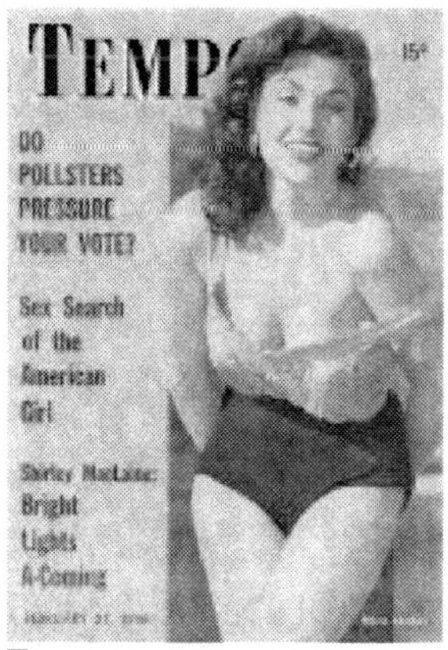

Tempo

Tempo

Temptee

That Girl...

Thigh High

'Skirts that flirt.'

Press Arts Inc., Canoga Park CA.

1967 – 1970? At least 13 issues.

Pictorials.

Tic-Toc

Sampson Publishing and Distribution Co., New York NY.

Black and white interiors, with color centerfolds.

Early 1960's. At least 4 issues produced.

Pictorials, nonfiction.

Tiger

Reynard Publications, Chicago IL.

May 1956 – July 1957. 7 issues.

Nonfiction, pictorials.

The first two issues – May and August, 1956 – are virtually identical, with the same cover but a different month listed on each.

Tiger (Quarterly)

Publisher's Development Corp., Skokie IL.

Summer 1967 – Winter 1977. 50+ issues.

Pictorials, nonfiction.

Not to be confused with an underground gay erotic magazine from the mid-60's.

Tiger Girl

1964. More than 1 issue published?

Black and white photos, with some incidental color.

Nonfiction, pictorials.

Tigress

1964 – 1967. 5+ issues.

Pictorials, nonfiction.

Tip Top

American Art Agency Inc., Hollywood CA.

1960 – 1970? 30+ issues.

Pictorials.

Titter

Titter Inc., New York NY.

Black and white interiors.

August 1943 – April 1955. 65 issues.

Pictorials, nonfiction.

Thigh High

Tic-Toc

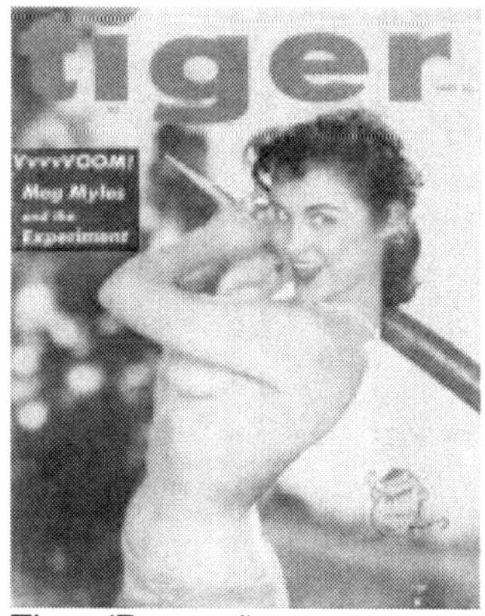

Tiger (Reynard)

Tiger (Pub. Dev.)

Tiger Girl

Tigress

Tip Top

Tip Top

Titter

TNT
Fax Publishing Co., Rockford IL.
Black and white interiors. Measures 4.5 by 6.5 inches.
Mid-1950's. How many issues published?
Pictorials, nonfiction, fiction.

Today's Breed
Seven Seventy Publishers, North Hollywood CA.
1960's. More than 1 issue published?

Tomcat
PURRsonality Publishing Co., Oakland CA.
Black and white interiors.
1956 – 1958. 6 issues.
Nonfiction, pictorials, cartoons.

Tomcat
Dominion Publishing Co., North Hollywood CA.
1969. 2 issues?
Pictorials, nonfiction.

Tomkat
International Publications Inc., Hollywood CA.
1962 – 1963? 6 issues?
Pictorials, nonfiction.

Tonight
American Art Agency, Hollywood CA (Parliament).
Black and white, and color photographs.
1959 – 1970? ~45 issues.
Pictorials.

Top Kicks
Anchor Publications, Gardena CA.
1965. How many issues produced?

Topper
Peerless Publishing Co., Los Angeles CA.
Black and white, and color photos.
July 1961 – 1980? 100+ issues plus several Annuals.
Nonfiction, pictorials, fiction.

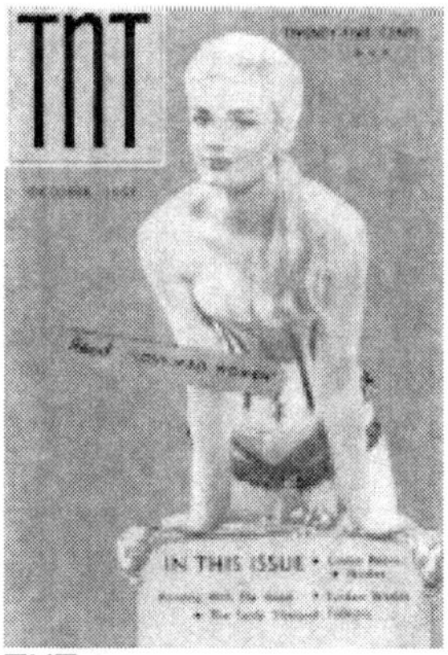

TNT

Tomcat (PURRsonality)

Tomcat (Dominion)

Tomkat

Tonight

Tonight

Top Kicks

Topper

Topper

Tops

J.B. Publishing Corp., New York NY.

Black and white interiors. Measures 4 by 6 inches.

March 1954 – January 1956. 18 issues?

Nonfiction, pictorials.

Torchy

Marst Publishing Co., North Hollywood CA.

1961 – 1966. 6 issues?

Pictorials.

Torchy

Seven Seventy Publishers, North Hollywood CA.

1960's. At least 2 issues published?

Torrid

Bodee Publications, Inc. (Roena Publications Inc., Los Angeles CA).

Black and white interiors.

1961. Only 1 issue published?

Pictorials, nonfiction.

This was probably put together from features cobbled together from other magazines.

Touch

Studio Publications / American Art Agency, Hollywood CA (Parliament).

1958 – 1970. 25+ issues.

Pictorials.

A magazine under the title *The New Touch* published by Jaybird Enterprises (basically the same company as American Art Agency) was published in the early 1970's, but wasn't necessarily a continuation of this title, so it isn't covered here.

Touch of Venus

Caesar Publishers Inc., New York NY.

Black and white interiors, with color centerfolds.

1962 – 1965. ~8 issues.

Pictorials, nonfiction.

There were also at least 3 calendars released also.

Triple-Length Adventure

Atlas Magazines Inc., New York NY.

April 1961. One-shot.

Adventure fiction.

Tops

Torchy (Marst)

Torchy (770)

Torrid

Touch

Touch

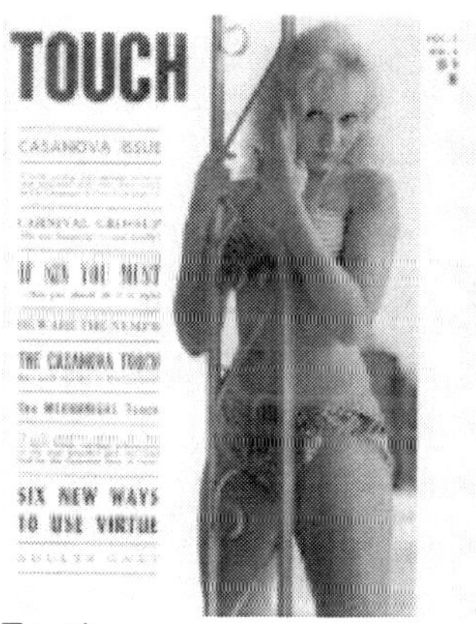

Touch

Touch of Venus

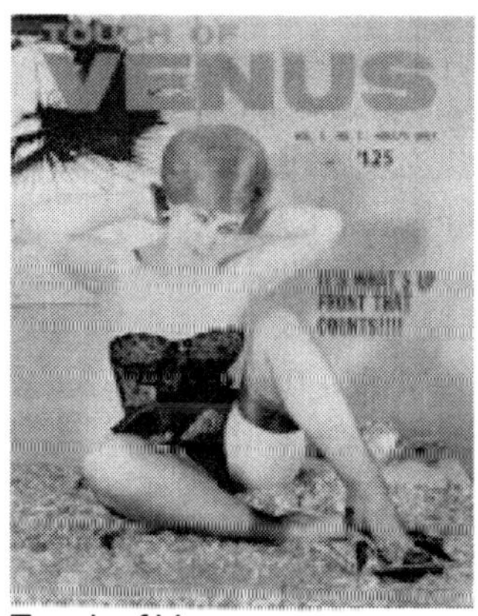

Touch of Venus

Trojan

American Art Agency, Hollywood CA (Parliament).

Black and white interiors, with some color photos.

1962 – 1969. ~30 issues.

Pictorials.

Note: v.1, #2's cover is identical to that of the one-shot *Celebrate* (see the entry for that title).

Tropical Paradise

Late 1950's? More than 1 issue?

True

Country Press Inc., Louisville KY; Fawcett Publications; Petersen Publishing.

June 1937 – 1976. 400+ issues, plus several Yearbooks.

Nonfiction, pictorials.

This was a magazine which, as the title suggests, was dedicated to compelling nonfiction articles. Toward the end it had devolved into a near-pornographic pictorial mag.

True Action

Official; Magazine Management (Atlas).

January 1959? – 1977? ~100 issues.

Fiction, nonfiction, pictorials.

True Adventures

New Publications.

September 1955 – 1971? 170+ issues.

Fiction, nonfiction, pictorials.

This is one of those adventure-fiction magazines that later transitioned to nude content in the early 70's.

Note: This was formerly the pulp *New Detective Magazine*.

True Battles of World War II

Stanley Publications Inc., New York NY.

November 1963 – June 1966. 12 issues.

Adventure fiction.

True Danger

See *Man's True Danger*.

True Men

Feature Publications, New York NY; Stanely Publications Inc., New York NY.

October 1956 – October 1974.

Fiction, nonfiction.

Trojan

Trojan

Tropical Paradise

True

True

True Action

True Adventures

True Battles of WWII

True Men

True Spy and War Stories
Jalart House, New York NY.
February 1966 – February 1967? 3 issues?
Nonfiction, fiction.
This magazine apparently used a lot of reprinted stories.

True War
Magnum Publications Inc., New York NY.
October 1956 – July 1958. 11 issues.
Fiction, nonfiction.

True War Stories
Westridge Publishing Corp., Cleveland OH.
January-February 1953. More than 1 issue?
Fiction, nonfiction, pictorials.

TV Girls and Gags
Enterprise Magazine Management, Atlanta GA.
Black and white interiors, with occasional color.
May 1954 – 1963. ~50 issues.
Cartoons, humor, pictorials.
This cheap little title was mostly cartoons, with some jokes and a few girlie photos thrown in.

Twilight
International Publications Inc., Hollywood CA.
Black and white interiors, with color centerfolds.
1962. More than 2 issues?
Pictorials, nonfiction.

Twilight (2nd)
Late 1960's – 1971? At least 13 issues produced.
Pictorials.

Ultra
Sari Publishing Co., North Hollywood CA.
Black and white interiors with color centerfolds.
1963 – 1967? ~15 issues produced.

Undie World
Winter 1963. More than 1 issue published?

Unique Illustrated
1965 – 1966? More than 3 issues published?
Pictorials, nonfiction, fiction.

True Spy and War Stories

True War

True War Stories

TV Girls and Gags

TV Girls and Gags

Twilight (2nd)

Ultra

Undie World

Unique Illustrated

Untamed
Magnum Publications Inc., New York NY.
February 1959 – March 1960. 8 issues.
Adventure fiction, nonfiction.

Vagabond (1st)
1959. More than 1 issue?
Pictorials, nonfiction.

Vagabond
Polo Publishing Co., Chicago IL.
1960 – 1961. 5 issues?
Nonfiction, pictorials.

Valor
Skye Publishing Co., New York NY.
June 1957 – December 1959. 13 issues plus 1 Annual.
Adventure fiction.

Valor
Charlton Publications, Derby CT.
November 1968 – March 1969. 3 issues.
Fiction, pictorials.

Varsity Annual
1963. One-shot?

Venus
Garden of Eve Publications Inc., New York NY.
Black and white interior.
1958 – 1960. 15 regular issues, plus 2 Annuals and at least 1 Calendar.
Fiction, pictorials, nonfiction.

Vivid Tales
Sari Publishing Co., North Hollywood CA.
1960 – 1961. 3 issues.
Pictorials, nonfiction, fiction.

Vixen
International Publications Inc., Hollywood CA.
1961 – 1963. 8 issues?
Pictorials.
Did issues v.1 #4 through v.1 #9 exist?
One of the extant issues is a 1961 'Special Edition' that may predate v1. #1.

Untamed

Untamed

Vagabond (1st)

Vagabond (Polo Pub.)

Valor (Skye)

Valor (Charlton)

Venus

Vivid Tales

Vixen

Voluptas
Sampson Publishing and Distribution Co., New York NY.
Black and white interiors. Measures 6 by 9 inches.
Early 1960's. More than 1 issue published?
Pictorials.

Voluptuous Vixens
Dante Publishing Co.
1950's. One-shot?

Vue
'America's photo digest.'
VUE Magazine Inc., New York NY.
Black and white interiors.
October 1950 – 1967? 100+ issues.
Pictorials, nonfiction.

War
Male Publishing, New York NY (Atlas).
1964 – 1968? 3-5 issues?
War fiction.

War Criminals
Normandy Associates, New York NY (Stanley).
August 1961 – December 1966. ~20 issues.
World War II nonfiction stories.

War Illustrated
Male Publications, New York NY (Atlas).
March 1964. One-shot?
War fiction.
Probably consisted of reprints from other Atlas magazines. Did this become *War*?

War Stories
Macfadden Publications.
Spring 1963 – Summer 1964. 4 issues.
World War II nonfiction stories.

War Story
Charlton Publications, Derby CT.
July 1957 – February 1959? ~10 issues?
World War II nonfiction stories.

Vue

Vue

Vue

War

War Criminals

War Criminals

War Illustrated

War Stories

War Story

Wench

Frimac Publications, North Hollywood CA.

1962. More than 1 issue?

Whirl

Actual Publishing Co.

1959. 4 issues.

Pictorials, nonfiction.

Whirl

1962. More than 1 issue?

Whisper

'The stories behind the headlines.'

Whisper Inc., New York NY.

Black and white interiors.

April 1946 – September 1953.

Nonfiction, fiction, pictorials.

This was largely a tabloid-style magazine that showcased plenty of non-nude cheesecake photos along with its more lurid articles and stories. It later turned into a straight-up gossip tabloid.

Did this turn back into a girlie magazine for its last several issues in 1969-1970?

Wicked

Tri-S Publications, Hollywood CA.

Black and white interiors, with color centerfolds.

1959 – ? At least 5 issues published.

Pictorials, cartoons.

Wild

October – December 1957. Only 2 issues?

Adventure fiction.

Wild Women

Health Knowledge Inc., New York NY.

Late 1960's – 1970? At least 13 issues.

Pictorials.

Wildcat (Adventures)

'Entertainment for men.'

Candar Publishing Co., New York NY.

June 1959 – 1976. ~80 issues plus several large-size Specials.

Adventure fiction, nonfiction, pictorials.

This magazine started its life as *Wildcat Adventures*, publishing men's adventure fiction; in 1965 it became a half-nudie pictorial girlie mag, just plain *Wildcat*.

Wench

Whirl (1959)

Whirl (1962)

Whisper

Whisper

Wicked

Wild

Wild Women

Wildcat

Wildcat (2nd)
1960's. How many issues were published?

Wink
'A whirl of girls.'
Wink Inc., New York NY.
Black and white interiors, with some color enhancements.
Summer 1944 – April 1955. 57 issues.
Pictorials.

Witch
Ken Publishing, Studio City CA.
1960's. More than 1 issue published?
Pictorials.

Wolf Bait
Zee Zee Publishing, New York NY.
1959. At least 2 issues published.
Pictorials, nonfiction.

Women in War
Normandy Associates, New York NY (Stanley).
1959 – 1964? More than 3 issues produced?
Adventure fiction.

Women of Intrigue
Art Enterprises Inc., Los Angeles CA.
1960 – 1965. More than 7 issues produced?
Pictorials, nonfiction, fiction.

Women of the World
Late 1960's. At least 2 issues produced.
This was a compilation magazine, made up of rebound issues of previous titles.

World of Men
EmTee Publishing, New York NY.
January 1963 – November 1973. 67 issues.
Adventure fiction, nonfiction, pictorials.
This title had some great covers from the beginning right up to the end.

Wow
Caesar Publishers Inc., New York NY.
1962. How many issues published?

Wildcat (2nd)

Wink

Wink

Witch

Wolf Bait

Women In War

Women Of Intrigue

Women of the World

World Of Men

X
'Xcitement in pictures.'
September 1956 – October 1957. 10 issues.
Nonfiction, pictorials.
Apparently this was a title change from something called *Anything Goes*.

Yes
American Art Agency Inc., Hollywood CA (Parliament).
Black and white interiors, with color centerfolds.
1961 – 1972? 10-15 issues published.
Pictorials.

Zest
Magtab Publishing, New York NY.
Black and white interiors. Digest sized.
May 1959 – April 1960. 6 issues.
Nonfiction, pictorials.
This was a temporary (for some reason) retitling of *Picture Scope*.

Zing
1960's. How many issues?

Zip
Humorama Inc., New York NY (Atlas).
Black and white interiors. Measures 5.5 by 7.5 inches.
1964 – 1972? 60+ issues published?
Cartoons, pictorials.

Zipper
Comet Publications, Los Angeles CA.
1960's. One-shot?

Zoftic
1960's. How many issues produced?

X

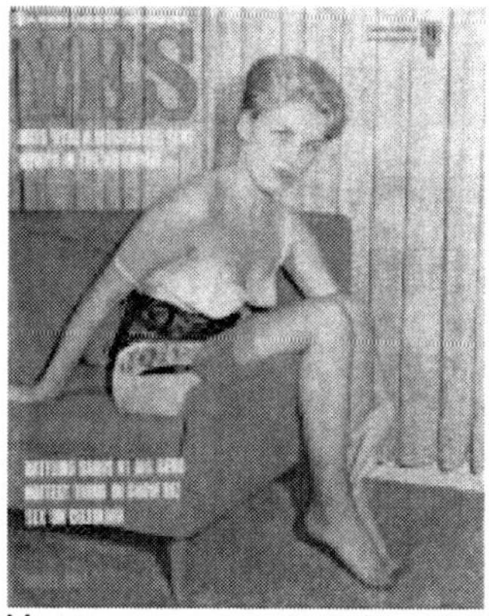

Yes

Zest

Zip

Zipper

Zoftic

Ordering Additional Copies

To order additional copies of this book directly from the author, send $24.95 (free shipping within the United States) for each copy to:

Todd Frye
PO Box 577
Harrogate TN 37752

Personal checks and money orders accepted.

To purchase via Paypal, or to make other shipping or quantity arrangements (including international purchases), please email the author at **toddfrye@yahoo.com**.

You might also be interested in one of my companion volumes:

The Vintage Trading Card Price Guide gives detailed information on over 400 vintage card and sticker sets from the years 1960 to 1985. Illustrated with over 320 photographs, this is the first trading card price guide released to the mass market in nearly 30 years. It is essential reading for collectors who want to discover the world of cards that existed long before any of the modern issues.

Retail is $24.95 with free shipping within the U.S.

The Complete Marvel Comics Visual Checklist features color cover images for *every* Marvel comic book published between 1939 and 1980, starting in this volume with titles A through L. That's over 4,800 cover images in this volume, plus additional information on each title.

Retail is $31.95 with free shipping within the U.S.

Retailers! To receive 50% off cover price, order at least 5 copies of any of these 3 books. You can mix and match: 2 copies of one, 2 of another, 1 of a third (for example). These are books that will be sought after by collectors of pop culture memorabilia. Immediate payment means shipping of books within 2 weeks.

Thanks!

CPSIA information can be obtained at www.ICGtesting.com
Printed in the USA
LVOW11s0538100414

381137LV00004B/22/P

9 780989 135436